CROSSING AND LIVING CULTURES

Annette Brunner

authorHOUSE®

AuthorHouse™ UK Ltd.
500 Avebury Boulevard
Central Milton Keynes, MK9 2BE
www.authorhouse.co.uk
Phone: 08001974150

First published by AuthorHouse   1/13/2011

ISBN: 978-1-4520-8260-8 (sc)
ISBN: 978-1-4520-8261-5 (hc)

This book is printed on acid-free paper.

Dedication

This book is dedicated to my son, Edgar, for enriching my life.

Contents

Acknowledgements

Thanks to all the people who were helpful during the writing of this book.

I would like to express my sincere thanks to my aunt Victoria Merz and my cousins Akwasi Poku and Diana Addai for giving me information on my Ghanaian family history.

I am most appreciative to my friends Beatrice Appiah-Kusi, Mercy Ananeh-Frempong, Charity Agyei-Amoama, Beatrice Aboley-Friebe, and my brother, Charles Brunner, for reading my drafts and providing useful information and criticism that contributed to this book.

Introduction

The aim of this book is to tell my son and future grandchildren and their children the story of my life: my roots and my journey through life.

This is a true story of crossing and living cultures. It shows the mixing of the races – European and African – and the cultural differences.

My maternal great-grandfather, Nana Kwame Kyem, was the chief of Bantama. His title was Bantamahene. In the past, Bantama was a village. Today, it is a suburb of Kumasi, in the Ashanti Region of Ghana. Nana Kwame Kyem is said to have been the last commander-in-chief of the last Ashanti army to have fought the British before colonial rule was established in Ashanti. Like his daughter, my grandmother Nana Akosua Kyem, he had no formal education and could neither read nor write. My educated mother, Agnes Abena Serwaa Boateng – whose father, Nana Boateng, was an Ashanti chief – married Europeans and had biracial children.

My father, Carl Albert Brunner, was Swiss, and I was born and raised in Ghana. I speak English, German, Twi, Swiss-German, and French. I am a German citizen through marriage, have a son, and have spent my adult life in Europe.

The white man's influence made me appreciate free speech,

and I was encouraged to ask questions that generally were frowned upon in Ashanti culture. Ashanti culture taught me patience. It taught me the importance of being able to compromise when necessary. Showing respect and exercising self-restraint during interactions were highly valued in this culture when I was growing up. So, these became my values as well.

I have travelled extensively in some parts of Africa, Europe, Asia, America, the Caribbean, Australia, New Zealand and the Fiji Islands. My journeys have fulfilled a deep-seated desire to learn about different cultures and peoples. Throughout my travels, some things kept becoming clearer about people and cultures. I realised that not only did many cultures have a lot in common but each culture has something unique to offer mankind. Throughout the ages, injustices were committed. People have used all kinds of causes and reasons to suppress those that were weaker – irrespective of colour.

Chapter One: Ghana

The story of my life would be incomplete without a brief account of Ghana.

The first British African colony to gain its independence was originally called the Gold Coast. The name was changed to Ghana after independence in 1957.

Ghana is a small English speaking African country on the west coast, bordering the Gulf of Guinea – only a few degrees north of the Equator. It is surrounded by the French speaking African countries of Ivory Coast to the west, Togo to the east, and Burkina Faso to the north.

Ghana has a land area of about 230,940 square km. Geographically, it is divided into three zones:

   a. The coastal belt along the Atlantic Ocean to the south is mostly low land with sandy beaches lined with coconut trees. The surf of the Atlantic Ocean is rough with wild, grey waves. Generally, the continental shelf is short, and this leads to a strong undercurrent, which pulls everything to sea. People avoid swimming in these parts. However, there are parts where the continental shelf is broad and the waves are gentler. People prefer to swim here. This has created a great respect by the inhabitants for the sea.

b. The forest belt in the middle of the country with its streams and rivers,

c. The savannah belt, where the land is covered by low-bush, park-like, dry, grassy plains, is in the north.

Ghana is divided into ten administrative units called regions. Accra, in the Greater Accra Region, is on the coast. It is the capital and largest city. Kumasi, in the forest-belt region of the Ashantis, is the second largest city. Tamale is the largest city in the north.

The climate is tropical – hot and humid – like the hottest season in Florida in the USA. Ghana, like many parts of Africa, chronically suffers from drought, causing water shortages in every part of the country. Red dust is everywhere. The heat and humidity wear one down, but there are a lot of sunshine and clear skies most of the year. Twelve months of the year is summer time, with slight changes of very dry and wet seasons.

Tropical rains are usually heavy but short with a lot of thunder and lightning. It rarely rains all day. Occasionally, it can rain continuously for three days. Everything comes to a halt when it rains. People run for cover and just sit out the storms inside, because you can get a thorough drenching even with umbrellas or raincoats. These rains can end as quickly as they start. Within half an hour, you can have dark, angry clouds, which bring rain, giving way to clear, blue, sunny skies. Rains, following dry spells, have caused major flooding, destroying roads, bridges, and homes.

Ghanaian history has been influenced through trade with the Arabs in the north and in the south through trade with European nations, like the Portuguese, Dutch, Danes, and the British.

The Europeans made trading posts and built castles on the coast to store their wares. These same storage spaces were used – years later – to store the more lucrative commodity of slaves.

Slavery among Ghanaian tribes existed long before the Europeans started the slave trade in Africa. Before the slave trade, captives taken during the many tribal wars in Ghana were kept as slaves. It also existed among my tribe, the Ashantis. My grandmother's family also had slaves. When the British conquered Ashanti, they abolished slavery. Many of these slaves remained with their old families. So it was with the slaves of my grandmother's family. To this day, their descendants are treated like family.

America, the New World and its plantations, created the need for a large work force and a destination for the slave trade. The Europeans encouraged the tribes of the African continent to sell men and women they took as prisoners in their tribal wars. For the Africans it meant not only wealth but also a means of getting rid of their enemies forever.

Another way of capturing slaves in Ghana was through the African subcontractors of the Arabs, Africans, and Europeans, whose custom it was to raid villages and force their people into slavery.

I remember being told about the past raids when I was small. It was a story about a mother and her child, from a village in the Ashanti Region. While this mother was pounding fufu – a pounded paste from boiled yam or plantain, and cassava – she heard drums warning them to go into hiding. Drums were used those days not only for music and dancing, but most of all, they were used to communicate to people. This was done so well that they were known as "the talking drums". As the story goes, in her panic, she picked up the fufu mortar instead of her toddler who was sitting right next to her. It was upon arriving at her safe hiding place that she realized her mistake. It was, of course, too late to go back for her child. She returned later to find it murdered. Like all raiders, they took what they wanted and left a lot of destruction behind. This story shows the great fear in which people lived during those times.

Friendly people

Ghana's Coast near the Elmina Castle.

The People

Ghanaians are known for their friendliness and ready smiles. Their hospitality makes every visitor feel the true meaning of *Akwaaba*, which means "welcome". It is a nation of many tribes with some cultural differences. Each tribe has its own language. The tribal groups are mainly the Gas and Ewes in the southeast; the Akans (to which the Ashantis belong) in the centre and south west; and the people of the northern region. Most people are black in complexion. Since the Europeans came to the south as early as the fifteenth century and the Arabs to the north – even much earlier – there has been a lot of miscegenation. Their legacy has been some fair-skinned people.

Ghanaians like to have large families. A family for the Akans includes parents, siblings, cousins, nephews, uncles, aunties, grandparents, and all blood relatives on the matrilineal side. There is no apparent distinction between the immediate and extended family. Parents and older people are treated with respect. As a result, most Ghanaians if they come to Europe are shocked by how older people are treated there. In Ghana, families offer help and support as need be. The idea is for those who can afford it to contribute to the needs of others who are less fortunate. Therefore, taking or receiving is seen as normal. Indeed, it is often expected and understood that the one with more should give to the less fortunate.

Most people do not have a pension, and because there is no proper pension scheme for the old, children are expected to help their parents financially. This is seen as "one good turn deserves another." Today, parental ties are still strong, but the ties of the extended families are not as close as they were in the past because the challenges of modern life make it impossible for people to provide financial support for all members of their extended families.

In comparison, the European family consists of only the nuclear family. European parents are usually only responsible for their children until the children become adults. Children are not expected to support their parents because of the better-developed pension scheme for the old.

Ghanaian women take pride in dressing up colourfully. The headgear usually matches the outfit, and this is artistically wrapped around the head in a most eye-catching manner. One-coloured materials are rare. Men find women with generous behinds sexy. Too thin or too slim is not desirable. A bit of flesh is appreciated. To have a flat abdomen is not considered a trait of beauty. There is no hurry. Slow walking is a sign of grace, and most young women pick this up at a very early age and with time they get even slower. Some women believe sports make a woman too musclebound and take away her womanliness.

People generally prefer warm meals and traditionally eat sometime in the course of the morning and in the evening. I read on the Internet, "Ghanaian cuisine is heavy with starch, generous on fat, and light on meat". It is true. Because of the lack of meat, if a meal has the meat on a bone, they love picking that bone clean. They also love chewing bones.

Typical dishes with their special soups and sauces are jollof rice, banku, kenkey, gari, kelewele, and the most popular dish – fufu. Jollof rice is rice cooked in a stew or sauce. Banku and kenkey are made from cornmeal dough. Gari looks like couscous, but is made from cassava. Kelewele is an all-time favourite snack sold on the streets of Ghana. It is cut-up ripe plantain, to the size of fingers, well seasoned, and deep-fried in oil.

Like many countries in Africa, many people still prepare their meals on open fires (with charcoal or wood) outside their dwellings, in the courtyard. Since this is on the ground, they sit on very low stools while they cook. For these people, meals are generally eaten while sitting on wooden stools or chairs, using small tables or none at all. Due to European influence and education, some people nowadays use modern kitchen equipment. They also eat European meals and dine in westernised dining rooms.

Traditionally, a spoon might be the only cutlery used for eating foods like porridge. Ghanaians usually eat with their right fingers. The left hand's function is for anything unclean. It is therefore not at all accepted to use the left hand to shake hands or receive or give anything to anyone. To do so is viewed as impolite. Only the right hand is to be used for pointing at anything.

Colonial Times

Prior to 1957, when Ghana became independent, there was a colour bar, but it was not as stringent as it was in South Africa. Europeans and Africans had separate wards in hospitals. Europeans had their own clubs, which were forbidden to blacks. The only blacks allowed there were the servants. Interracial marriages were not expressly forbidden but were not accepted by Europeans, especially the British. European society, in Ghana tolerated white men living with black women, either as mistresses or through native marriages. A white that officially and legally married a black was looked down upon in the white community. So, before independence, white men were usually not prepared to marry a black by the ordinance. However, a few brave Europeans, mainly from the continent, were courageous enough to dare to break this unwritten convention. Many British people also followed suit after independence.

A relationship between a white woman and an African man was breaking the worst taboo. She was socially lynched by the Europeans. In the African world, she was respected, but she lived in isolation. This was often due to lack of common interests with the African women. Besides, most African women then were not educated.

Ghanaian women married to Europeans said they were discriminated against. When European visitors entered their homes, the wives were not even acknowledged. Should they visit European homes with their husbands, they were just ignored and not offered a seat. They could choose to stand unnoticed and snubbed next to their partners or join the household servants.

My mother told me that once she and John (our English stepfather) decided to test the colour bar. They went to the British Club in Kumasi but were turned away by the African guards at the entrance. The excuse was that they were not members. The following day, John went there alone, and he was allowed in. He never went there again until after independence when the colour bar was lifted.

It was not only Europeans who frowned upon mixed couples. Some Ghanaians did also, and they did not hide their feelings. My mother said once she and John went to a hot spot called Hotel de Kingsway in Kumasi. As they went outside to their car, one of the taxi drivers waiting for a customer made it clear he disapproved of interracial relationships and proceeded to heckle them. John, an ex-army officer from the Second World War who was normally phlegmatic, lost his temper and punched the man in the chest. This driver fell down heavily, then ran back to the other taxi drivers, exhorting them to help him beat up the white man. They demurred. Being practical people, they told him in no uncertain terms that they were there to make money, not to get into fights. This being still the colonial era, they did not fancy going to prison for beating up a white man, especially one of our colonial overlords. From prison, they could not support their families.

The Europeans in Ghana saw a biracial child as a love child. They were looked upon as exotic and unusual because of the lighter colour of their skin and their more Caucasian features. These children were referred to by both races as "mulattoes", "mixed race", "half-castes", and at times, as "coloureds". Biracial children raised by white fathers were usually raised to value mainly European culture. Their black heritage was considered inferior, so that part of their heritage was left untaught. In fact, some were discouraged from speaking the African languages and grew up unable to speak the local languages – just like their white fathers. However, biracial children were not always completely accepted by the European community – be it in Ghana or in Europe – because they were not white.

Ghanaians accepted biracial children, admiring their light skin colour. Should they appear in an area where they were a rare species – such as in a village or poorer part of town – people stopped whatever they were doing and looked. If you were in a car, they surrounded the car and stared, commenting to each other. Should you leave your car, they followed you, saying to one another phrases such as: "look at her feet"; "look at her hair"; "look at her eyes"; "look at her mouth"; and so on. You were for that moment the centre of attention. For us, it was uncomfortable. At times, they called us derogatory names.

In Ghana, among the Akans, white people are referred to as "Oburoni". Akans also refer to Arabs and Asians as "Oburoni". Paradoxically, they also refer to biracials as "Oburoni".

Biracial children were thought of, by Ghanaians, as privileged and were expected to act that way. Because of their half-white backgrounds, they were expected to be better off financially in the society with standards equal or almost equal to that of the Europeans. This was unreasonable. Most biracial children did not live privileged lives, because they grew up without their white fathers. They were often products of short or secret affairs. Most Europeans were sent down to Ghana as expatriates, with or without their wives, with short contracts that limited their stay in the country. Sometimes, their relationships were of short duration, and the men were not even aware that the women had taken seed. The men and women would part, never to see one another again, when the men's contract expired. So, the women were left alone to fend for their biracial children, often in a position of financial difficulty. Should these children not be able to live up to these expectations, however, and live at the same level as the locals, they were openly ridiculed by some.

Growing up then as products of these two races always posed challenges for the mixed-race child. The biracial child had the burden of finding a stable position between the two cultures. Some did. Some managed. But others did not. For some biracial children, these challenges resulted in feelings of confusion, which many struggled with throughout their lives.

I felt pretty grounded growing up in the two cultures, in a home with two parents of different races. I remember the warmth and love I felt whenever I was among my Ashanti relatives and friends. I also felt at ease with my parents' European friends. Looking back, I felt I had freedom – then and now – which always allowed me to be myself. Some biracial children, like me, grew up knowing and appreciating both cultures. For most, the influence of the local culture was greater, because they grew up without a white father's influence.

MY BIRACIAL FAMILY

Abena Serwaa (my Ashanti mother)

1st husband – Carl Albert Brunner (Swiss)   2nd husband – John Anthony Knuckey (English)

Charles, Maurice & Annette   Brenda & Caroline

My father

Chapter Two: My Beginnings

My Father

My father, Carl Albert Brunner, was born on 3 November 1916 in the town of Balsthal in the Swiss German Canton (State) of Solothurn. In Ghana, he was known as Charles Albert, which is what appears on our birth certificates – Charles, Maurice, and me. He died at the age of thirty five from polio. It is said he died within weeks of contracting the disease. Evidently, the polio had affected his respiratory system. This was on 4 November 1951, in Casablanca, a few months before I was born. Morocco at that time was a French colony. He was on his way back to Ghana after a trip to Switzerland. His only sister, Tante Alice, told me years later in Switzerland that he often complained of pain in his leg. No one took it seriously as it was expected to go away. And so, our father made his return trip back to Ghana, via Casablanca, in a country he always swore he would see before he died.

In Ghana, people remember him as having charisma. They also say he had a friendly disposition. His friends said he had a good sense of humour and was warm hearted and generous. Our mother told us he was a good husband, a loving father, and a generous person. People that worked with him knew where they stood. He was a fearless, straightforward, no-nonsense type of a man. He stood six feet tall, was left handed, and an expert at ju jitzu, the Japanese martial art of self defence. This served him well, living in camps in the rough, untamed, jungle environment. The people that he sometimes encountered were not always friendly. The ease with which he disarmed and bashed up opponents who dared to pull a knife or a cutlass on him won him both respect and fear.

He first came to Ghana (then known as Gold Coast) in the late 1930s. He was an accountant by training and worked in this capacity for SCOA (Societe Commerciale de L'Ouest Africain), a French-owned international distribution company. Later, he went to work for and became the partner of one Chatelain, a Swiss-French, who was a general contractor in the Western Region of Ghana. They built roads and were in the timber business as well. As he was the life and soul of the company, the firm went rapidly downhill after his death. Chatelain was an old man who was in very bad health. I understand he died not long afterward.

Their business was run like this: they would take a concession, fell the trees, then move on. Thus, they kept on moving from camp to camp, like nomads. If they could find a house with enough space to store their materials and trucks, then they would rent it as they did in Huni Valley. Mostly, however, they rented a piece of land from the chiefs on which they built a large camp of wood and coconut branches. At least two snakes were found and killed each day in these primitive living quarters. The snakes were escaping from their predators, but people and snakes do not mix. They are nervous creatures, apt to strike without warning, and their bite can be fatal. The amenities were very basic as the following story shows.

My brother Charles says when he was about four years of age he lived in the bush with our parents and Dede, our mother's maid, who doubled as his nanny as well. Charles was not allowed to use the pit latrine the adults used, because he was too small. To relieve himself, he had to go to the bush during the day. At night, he used the chamber pot under his bed. One day, he had a strong urge to go in the bush. In the careless way of all children, he did not bother to look around first. After he finished his business, he heard a noise behind him. He turned and there was this black cobra shedding its skin. He became petrified with shock and fright. He could not move. He started screaming. Mama sent Dede over, but she ran away when she saw the snake. Finally, Mama herself came and pulled Charles away. Knowing how frightened our mother was of snakes, it was very courageous of her, but then, when your child is in danger you throw caution and fear to the winds. At that time, Charles was an only child.

At work, trying to build up a company was not easy either. This was during the struggle for independence in the 1940s. Nationalists burned down the company's sawmill and our father planned to rebuild the mill after things had settled down.

At one point, our father was supervising the repair of a road that had been washed away by the tropical rains. In one of the passenger lorries that had stopped on the other side of the road was an agitator. Upon seeing a white man and an African audience he decided to put on a show. He started berating our father about the ills of the white man and what they were going to do to Europeans in Ghana after independence. Finally, our father could not take it anymore, so he lifted the agitator up and threw him into the ditch beside the road. The man shut up immediately and crept back into the lorry like a dog with his tail between his legs. The audience were relieved that the white man took care of the troublemaker and could get back to his work so they could finally continue their journeys.

Our father was gifted in languages. He spoke French, Swiss-German, High German, and English. He grew up in the Swiss-French-speaking town of Bienne, so he regarded himself as a French speaker. His mother was also Swiss French. He never forgave his father, who was Swiss German, for divorcing her when she was diagnosed with terminal throat cancer. Because of his French accent, he pronounced Charlie "Sharlie", a pronunciation still used by all our cousins and even by our mother occasionally. Unusual for a white then, he spoke good Twi (the language of the Ashantis) and a smattering of other local languages such as Hausa, Dagati, and Nzema.

His sudden death left my twenty-five-year-old Ghanaian mother, Abena Serwaa, alone to raise my two brothers, Charles and Maurice, and me.

My mother later met an Englishman, John Anthony Knuckey. They married and spent the rest of their lives together. John was also initially in the timber business, and we lived in my mother's house in Kumasi, a town in the Ashanti Region of Ghana. Working in the timber business meant spending long periods of time in the dense forests of this region. They were away a lot. In their absence with our little half sisters – Brenda and Caroline Knuckey – our Ashanti grandmother, Akosua Kyem, became the caretaker of Maurice and me – no small feat. Charles was then in boarding school at the coast in St Augustine's Secondary (High) School.

We were lively children. We were curious, daring, and adventurous. As we were her grandchildren, she spoilt us and allowed us more liberties than we could handle. We were happy and felt free. We lived close to nature. The outdoors was ours, and we were busy exploring and enjoying it. Unlike most Ashanti children, we were not discouraged in these exploits. Being in charge of us was therefore a big task for a traditional middle-aged Ashanti lady who could not keep up with us.

My grandmother, Nana Akosua Kyem, on the left

My Grandmother, Nana Akosua Kyem

I was known as Akosua Kyem Nana – which is Twi for Akosua Kyem's grandchild (girl or boy). My grandmother was a petite, dark, slim Ashanti woman with fine features. Everything about her was slim and fine. Her hands and limbs were slim and fine. The only thing that stood out on her was her behind. It was so prominent you wondered how her delicate legs could support such weight. I did not know that it was considered very sexy and desirable in her culture. I concentrated on those huge eyes of hers, hidden behind her thick Coke-bottle type lenses.

Like most Ashantis, she was very clean in her person. Cleanliness was an obsession. Bathing twice a day was a must. She had a habit of getting our bath water ready in a bucket and then announcing to our utter embarrassment, in front of visitors, that we should go and bath. Oral hygiene was also an obsession. Like most people of her generation, she never used a toothbrush or toothpaste. They used a special chewing stick. Her chewing stick was part of her. She removed it only to eat, to bath and to go to bed. Otherwise, there was a constant chewing and brushing of her good strong teeth. Occasionally, she would spit out, in an arrow form, the accumulated saliva. I have never seen anyone that could spit with such precision. I guess that was from years of practice. She hated dirty surroundings, a trait shared by my mother and her brother. She did not mind getting down and dirty; in other words, she did not shirk work.

Nana (grandma) followed the *densinkran* fashion. The *densinkran* fashion was the two-piece, traditional dress (like togas) of Ashanti queens. Therefore, to differentiate queens from the ordinary women who chose this fashion, the latter were not allowed to wear the traditional sandals that go with it. They went barefoot. Only queens were allowed to wear the traditional sandals with the *densinkran* fashion.

However, for the normal and ordinary fashion practised by most young women, the two-piece cloth and the matching top known as *kaba* were worn, and anyone could put on any type of footwear.

Nana Akosua Kyem also sported the popular *densinkran* hairstyle for women. The *densinkran* hairstyle was a close-cropped, neat haircut with the sides neatly razor trimmed. For the hair colouring, women scraped the fine soot that covered the bottom of the open-fire cooking pots. This was mixed with hair pomade and rubbed into the hair to give it that black look and shine.

This hairstyle was preferred by Ashanti women after menopause. It made them look like men, and they actually acted like men since they were consulted by the men and their advice was well respected. They were behind-the-scenes power movers and matchmakers. They were a force to reckon with in traditional society.

Nana had a varied and interesting social life. She belonged to many local clubs (known as *kuo* in Twi) dealing with female matters. She was a good dancer and belonged to the women's *Adowa* club, where she was a high-up. Charles still remembers them meeting several times at Nana's place in Ashanti New Town and later at Mama's house. Their leader was known as *Adowahemaa*, literally queen of *Adowa* dancers. Nana regularly attended funerals, which are normally colourful and important social events in Ashanti. At cultural ceremonies, Nana's performance and interpretation of the Ashanti *adowa* dance mesmerized on-lookers. In this communicative dance she would provoke rivals, flirt, and show off, in turn.

I recall once Nana came back from one of her club meetings beside herself with excitement. That usually meant she had some juicy gossip to tell us, and we were not disappointed. Nana and her club members had had a public meeting at Abbey's Park in Kumasi. It was apparently an emotional gathering, and one of the speakers, a friend of Nana's, got a bit carried away and bore down too hard while talking. The result was catastrophic. She broke wind. It was long and loud. The loud noise was heard all over the park. She was mortified. In the stunned silence that followed, she slunk off the podium and left the park very quickly. She dropped out of sight completely, and we never saw her again at Nana's place. For weeks on end, Nana talked about nothing else, embellishing it as she went on. Unfortunately, a budding career in women's causes came to an abrupt and rather explosive end for this friend.

My hair type was different, and Nana did not know what to do with it. It was too long, in her eyes, and it took too much care to keep it neat. It should be close cut like hers, as she would often complain to my mother. She was not totally wrong, for I was a tom-boy, not vain, and hated brushing my soft hair. When she saw me sitting still, she never tired of saying to my mother: "Now is the perfect time for Annette to receive a *densinkran* hair cut. My *Yiwan* (the Ashanti word for razor) is available". My mother just ignored her. Mama was proud of her daughter's soft, wavy European hair.

Ashantis were traditionally warriors, farmers, craftsmen, and traders. They were feared as warriors. My friend, Beatrice Appiah-Kusi explained to me, that the Ashanti war formation was adopted from ants on the march. This was improved upon as time went on. Horse riding was unknown to them, and so they went on foot as warriors. This had the advantage that they could hide in the forests and surprise their opponents, who had their officers on horseback, like the warriors from the northern region of Ghana and later, the British. The military adventures of the Ashantis led to tribal wars, which eventually led to the Ashantehene (Ashanti king) becoming the overlord of extended areas beyond the Akan speaking tribes of Ghana. In big wars, when all the head chiefs had to appear in person, the army was commanded by the Bantamahene (the chief of Bantama). Each body of men, led by its chief, went to war with its own supply of ammunition, its own reserve of food rations, and its own medicine men. The commander-in-chief communicated with the various bodies of troops by means of special runners and talking drums and received news of the progress of the battle in like manner.

Nana was once a trader. She had good business acumen, a trait inherited by Maame Abena Asubonteng, her oldest child. In her younger days, Nana often travelled to the north to buy yams, and other goods and returned to sell the items in Kumasi. She had a stall in the Central Market at *Kejetia*. A distant relative, Akua Nimah, inherited this after Nana's death, a decision her children did not contest because of Akua Nimah's devoted service to Nana over the years. Akua Nimah was given at a young age by her mother to Nana, to be brought up by Nana, who was well-off. Still today, this is a common practice in Ghana.

My grandmother sold yams in the market during the day. In the evenings, she sold roasted yams and plantains under a street light that was in front of her house. This was to make sure that all the items got sold before they got rotten. She also offered *tatre*. *Tatre* is pounded, ripe plantain deep-fried in palm oil, a delicacy loved by Ashantis young and old. Nana had a good location and, everything else being equal, was successful until she became a grandmother. Mama and her sister's children used to go to her for freebies. Finally, Nana gave up, because her grandchildren were not only eating away her profits, her principal was becoming affected. Poor Nana! She could not bring herself to deny her inconsiderate grandchildren and their friends.

People, throughout the ages, in every part of the world, have believed in some form of an almighty power. Before Christianity reached the Ashantis, they were animists. They believed in spirits and served one god through other smaller gods, which were represented by natural things like rivers, trees, rocks, and statues. Each of these smaller gods had their respective priest or priestess who intervened on behalf of their people.

It became fashionable during Nana's time to be a Christian and get a Christian name as well. Like most family members, she was an Anglican. Nana's baptismal name was Mary. Although nominally a Christian, she still believed in the old animist religion of the Ashantis and regularly went to her village, Patase, to consult the gurus. She simply added the Christian God and his cohorts to the Ashanti gods, so she saw no conflict of interest. As far as she was concerned, she was protecting herself two-fold.

In Patase, there was a self-declared witch called Maame Apoaa, who was a soothsayer, herbalist, and juju woman. She cast spells on people and freed others from spells. Nana used to visit her regularly and even for a while enticed our mother to accompany her when life was not going well for her. Once, Nana had a chicken killed as an offering to the gods and said prayers to the ancestors in Mama's house in Kumasi. I have forgotten why.

Nana spoke her mind and never beat about the bush about anything. She was very blunt and called a spade a spade. Nana could be abusive and obnoxious, but she had a heart of gold. There was no situation or problem she would not jump in to confront. In fact, her first reaction to a provocation was, "Let me also give it to them". This set her on her usual warpath, armed with a formidable weapon – her tongue. It was sharp and dreaded, for she had a high command of words in her language, Twi.

She would tactfully start the altercation by first swearing the Great Oath of the Ashantis known as *Ntam Kesse* and summoning the gods and ancestors on her side to witness the wrong that was being done to her. They were to see how intensely she was being provoked and sorely tested by the offenders. They were also to witness this confrontation of words and not of fists! Under no circumstances was it a physical confrontation. Nana's utterances put the necessary fear in her opponents, which made them realise that not only were the gods keenly paying attention to the verbal war, but had probably taken sides against them already. In a superstitious society, this worked like magic, and Nana had a field day each time!

Ashantis are a proud race with a high sense of personal dignity. Nana was a true Ashanti. She was authentic all the way. Her children called her, *Eno*, meaning "mother", and all her grandchildren called her, *Nana*, meaning "grandmother". She lived her life the way she wanted. After two marriages and four children, three of whom survived, she decided marriage was not for her, but that was not to deprive her of the company of men.

Ashantis believed in the sanctity of their tribal customs. My grandmother understood her culture. She was very well versed in Ashanti court etiquette, because she spent so many of her formative years at her father's court. She also had a healthy regard for other cultures. She never used the derogatory words some used against other tribes. In fact, she once scolded my brother Charles for using *Tani* in referring to one of our servants. *Tani* is a rude way of referring to someone from the northern region. Nana had reason to be proud as an Ashanti.

MY ASHANTI LINEAGE

Ama Ntosoa

1st husband *

2nd husband **Nana Kwame Kyem (Bantama chief)**

Bremawuo Sarpong (daughter)   **James Adjeikyem**   &   **Akosua Kyem (my grandmother)**

husband *   Had 2 wives   1st husband Akwasi Ofori   &   2nd husband **Nana Boateng (Patase chief)**

Sophia Okpeke & Kwaku Afriyie   Many children   **Abena Asubonteng**   **George** & Ama (died young) & **Abena Serwaa (my mother)**

Robert Okpeke (husband)   Twice married   Twice married   Twice married

* Names unknown   11 children   8 children   5 children

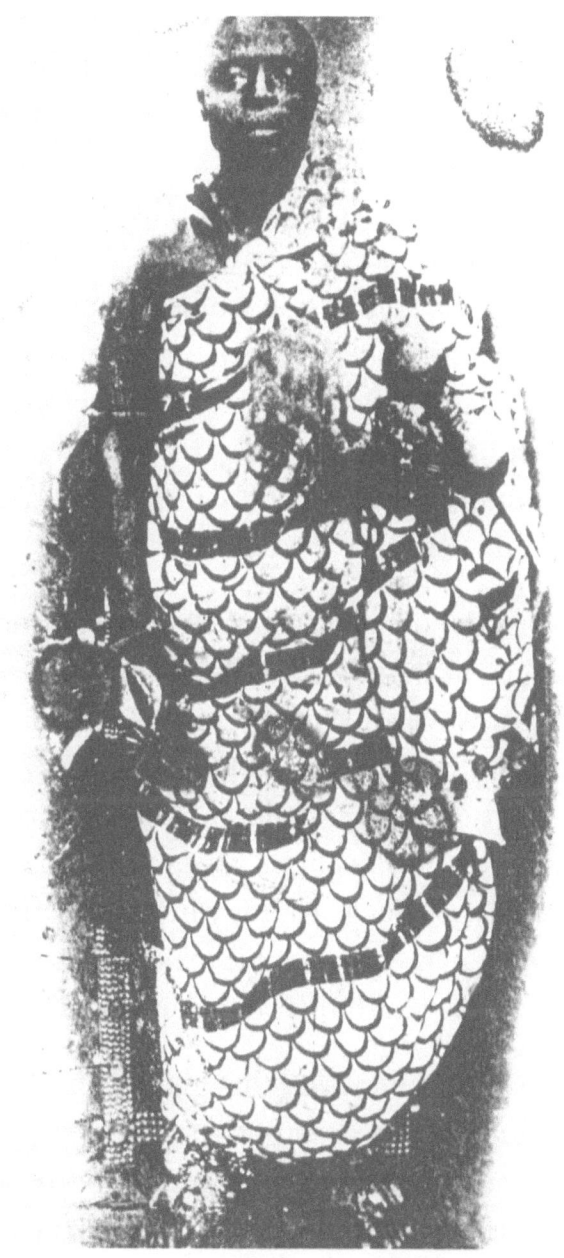

My great grandfather, Nana Kwame Kyem

She, after all, was the daughter of Ama Ntosoa and Nana Kwame Kyem. Nana Kwame Kyem was Bantamahene and Kontihene of the Golden Stool of Ashanti. The Golden Stool (covered with pure gold) represented the spiritual unity of the Ashantis, and their allegiance and loyalty to the Asantehene. Asantehene is the King of the Ashantis. The Kontihene is one of the key decision makers in choosing the Asantehene. The Bantamahene was also one of the senior commanders of the Ashanti army. Even though the Ashantis have a matrilineal system and Akosua Kyem really came from the Ama Ntosoa line, she and her brother claimed to come from the lineage of their father, Nana Kwame Kyem, because he was a powerful person in Ashanti society at the time.

The Ashantis practice of the matrilineal system meant that the children belonged to the mother's family. The child's alliance and commitment was to the mother's family. The children of a man were not his heirs. This meant when a father died, the inheritance went to his sister's children, who are nephews, not to his own children. His nephews were to inherit from him, and his own children belonged to his wife's family. Today, this belief and system rarely exists. People make wills to determine how they want their wealth distributed after their death.

One of the Ashanti customs was that guards were sent out to cut off heads when a chief or important member of the royal families in Ashanti died. The royal persons were supposed to be accompanied by people who would serve them in their life after death, thus the need to behead them. However, the guards made sure that the victims were not members of important families in Ashanti, who were known by their lineage. Non-Ashantis, who had performed some essential services to the Ashanti kingdom, were also exempted from being killed to accompany Ashanti VIPs to the underworld.

After years of lobbying by the missionaries, the British colonial rulers banned all such practices and declared them illegal. This only drove the practice underground. I am told it still happens but not as openly as in the past. However, the practice of identifying yourself through your lineage has remained with the older generation. When I was a child, it was stressed to me to always answer to the question of what my name was, "I am called Annette, Akosua Kyem's granddaughter," even if she was standing next to me. All of Nana's grandchildren had to also identify themselves as Akosua Kyem's granddaughter or grandson.

Ashantis were named according to the day of the week they were born. Males born on Mondays were called Kwadwo, females Adwoa; on Tuesdays, for males Kwabena and females Abena; on Wednesdays, males were named Kwaku and females Akua; males born on Thursdays were called Yaw, females were called Yaa; Kofi was the name for males born on Fridays and females were Afua; males born on Saturdays were Kwame and females were Ama; males born on Sundays were named Akwasi, and females Akosua.

Traditionally, in addition to the day names, Ashantis were named after an ancestor. Let us take the example, Akosua Kyem. "Kyem" was the name of one of her ancestors.

During colonialism, the British introduced the concept of surnames and first names. If a parent wanted to register a birth or a child at school, the government or school official demanded the father's name as surname and a first name. Most Christian officials demanded a Christian name. The parent had to make up a name or the official gave the boy or girl a Christian name. This situation still persists. The outcome has been that many people have two different sets of names: one for school and other official settings and another for the home and among friends. For example, someone's traditional given name may be Kwame Boateng; at school and at work, he may be known as John Mensah, Mensah being the name of his father.

According to Ashanti custom, it is the father who names the children. Our father being European gave us European names. His first born, Charles, was named after him, and to differentiate the two, Charlie was his son's pet name. Maurice, his second born, was named after his best friend in Ghana who was a French Algerian. He told my mother that should the third born be a girl, then he would name her Annette (after an old Swiss girlfriend of his). When I was born posthumously, my mother fulfilled his wishes and named me Annette. Nana was used to Ashanti names and had a problem pronouncing our European names. Annette was pronounced with an accent on the last letter – *Annette'*. It was the only name she could pronounce fairly well. She pronounced Charlie, *Sede*; Maurice was *Mrose*; Brenda was *Brana*; and Carol was *Kawro*.

My grandmother never saw the inside of a classroom. She was illiterate but full of folk wisdom. Like many of the older generation elite in Kumasi she adopted a lot of English words, but the pronunciation was such that no English person could understand what was being said. We had many laughs at her attempts at wrestling with English words.

It was also amusing watching her cope with modern appliances. I remember when he moved in with us, John Knuckey, our stepfather, brought a small electric stove with two ranges. Nana could never get the hang of it. She would always try fanning it into action as one would do with a charcoal grill, known in Ghana as a coal pot. Her forgetfulness as she got older was also a source of hilarity for us. I still remember her looking for a comb and berating us children for hiding it, when all the time it was under her armpit.

Nana called her girlfriends *Obaa*, meaning "woman", instead of calling them by their real names. They had a special way of communicating woman to woman. It was unique and entailed the use of words and body language that only they understood but that would baffle an outsider. It could be the way the shoulder was held. The special way of moving only their upper bodies from side to side, in a rhythmic way, without moving the rest of their bodies – whether they were sitting or standing – to add emphasis to what they were saying. It could also be the way the head was cocked or a facial movement. When it came to recounting their ailments, each did their best to out do the other. Nana could out act anyone, and I joined in her game sometimes.

There was an old mango tree in our garden. Often perched on one of its ample branches, I would be the one to spot visitors long before their arrival. I therefore had the advantage over my grandmother (who was often inside the house) of seeing one of her friends moving towards our house. I would rush inside and alert her, answering any other questions she might have about her approaching visitor.

"Nana, Nana, your friend is coming to visit you".

"Who is it?" started her quick interrogation, in her deep voice.

Since they always called each other *Obaa* (woman), I never knew their names.

"I don't know her name, Nana, but she is that fair-skinned friend of yours with the *densinkran* hairdo who was here not long ago. It is the one with a gap between her front teeth".

It clicked. She knew who it was.

"How far is she from the house?" was her next and final question.

"She is moving close to the big *Odum* tree just next to our house".

Eno immediately adopted a new posture. Suddenly she could not stand up straight anymore. Bent over as if in pain, moaning and groaning with the "mmmmmm's" and "aaaahhhhh's" of old age, she would pretend she had not been expecting any visitors. It would even take her a while to first acknowledge their presence. Eventually, she would go through the motions of recognising them and then say, "mmmmm! *Obaa*, my backache is worse than ever". Her friend would then reply, "Akosua, it's not you alone, ooooohhhh".

This friend would also list her aches and pains. Nana would continue narrating all her imaginary pains.

Eno was in her element. Behind this curious facade was her need to be the centre of attention. What else was there to be excited about? What else was interesting in her life? She had become an expert in creating scenes. When she was bored and maybe depressed, she would often say, *"Ewuo eme fa me"*

– meaning, "death come take me". We never believed her. We used to tease her that she would be the first to run away should the grim reaper actually appear!

Nana Akosua Kyem sowed some seeds in me during the couple of years I was to spend with her during my childhood. She was wise and often spoke in proverbs. At the time, I found her sayings sweet and amusing. Years later, as I reached adulthood, I was to find myself repeating these proverbs in difficult phases of my life to enable me find patience, tolerance and acceptance.

Here are some of my grandmother's philosophical sayings:

1. As a tree gets old, it develops a hole in its stem.
    (People develop physical weaknesses with age.)
2. Every negative state has its positive side.
    (Every cloud has a silver lining.)
3. Do not expect someone to keep your secret.
    (A secret is only a secret when you do not share it.)
4. Everyone has their monkey ways. (No one is perfect.)
5. Stones would have grown hairs by the time he takes action.
    (A lazy person postpones what needs to be done.)
6. With patience you can dissect an ant and find its liver.
    (With patience everything is possible.)
7. White people's food is ghost food.
    (It's not hot and spicy.)

8. I asked you to accompany me, and now you are leading me.

   (Using surreptitiously acquired information for self benefit; double-crossing in business deals)

9. I am a chamber pot. My name was ruined abroad before I got there.

   (You are disliked long before people get to meet you when your name is ruined)

10. Elders at home should sort out problems and not create them.

11. When a bird does not fly it is unable to find food.

    (There is a price to be paid for everything.)

12. A hunter does not always bring game home each time.

    (In life you sometimes win and sometimes lose.)

13. A thief is on the run long before he is chased.

    (A bad conscience knows no peace.)

14. Raising a fool is more difficult than giving birth to one.

15. When eyes run with tears, the nose follows too.

    (When you are in pain or trouble, it is the people who love you who share your pain.)

One day, Nana left Mama's house forever because she felt lonely and was having anxiety attacks. Our home in Krofofrom was lonely for her. She missed her compound setting in Ashanti New Town. So she just moved in with her older daughter there. Mama and John had left Kumasi for a while, and Nana just decamped, leaving us there. Fortunately, being in Africa, the relatives rallied around and helped us out until our parents returned. Mama was very angry but, given what we know now, it was the onset of dementia.

With the increasing years, she became weaker, and her eyesight started to fade. In time, she did not even recognise us. She later lost her mind. Nana became totally dependent on her children. To see someone previously so vibrant reduced to such a pathetic state was sad, and for those of us who loved her very painful. She died in 1968. Although she is long gone, we continue to remember her with affection. *Eno* still fills us with laughter and amusement when we think of her antics and her sayings.

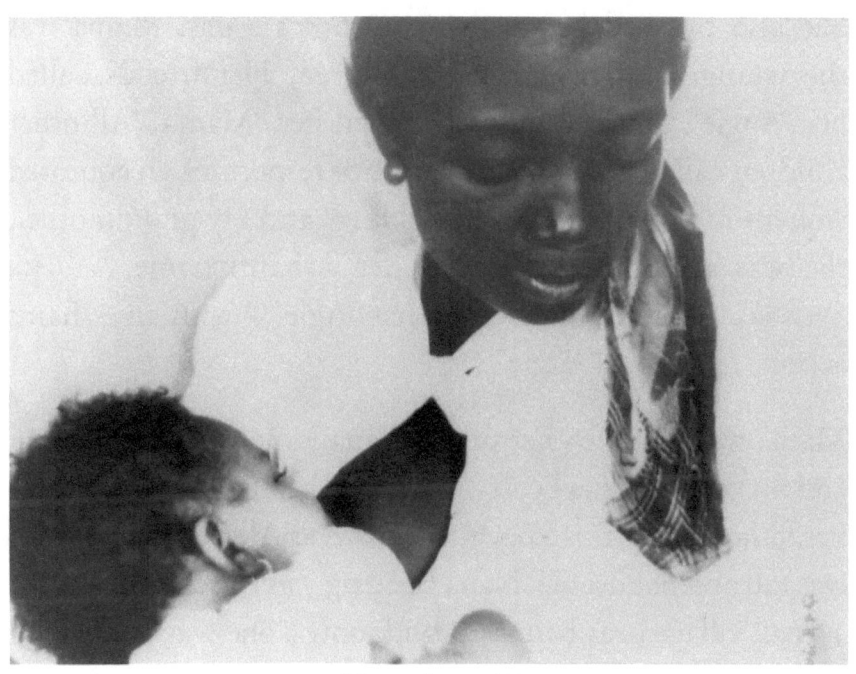

My mother and I

My Mother, Agnes Abena Serwaa Boateng

My mother, Agnes Abena Serwaa Boateng, was small in statue – like her mother, Nana. Although small, she had long legs. She was dark and pretty, with fine features and with kind gentle and unassuming manners. Like Nana, she was fussy about cleanliness, both personal and in her surroundings. She also brushed her teeth many times a day. Mama was the youngest of Nana's four children. Her friends called her "Aggie", and her children, called her "Mama". All other children called her "Auntie", a title of respect for an educated woman in Ashanti. With her siblings and my grandmother, she was sometimes called by her Ashanti name, "Abena Serwaa". At times, they called her "Agje" – with an Ashanti accent, meaning, "Aggie".

Mama was raised by her uncle, Nana James Yaw Adjeikyem, and his wife, Akosua Foah (*Kwaayie*). Therefore, I hardly knew her father, Nana Boateng, also known as Akwasi Nkore, who was tall and handsome. Nana Boateng was the chief of Patase, a small village near Kumasi – with only a one-way road going through the village. My mother had five biracial children. We were fully accepted by her extended family, as is the way of the Ashantis. Blood relations are important to them.

All the latter nearly did not happen. There were special homes in Ashanti from which the Asantehene could choose a wife. The girl had to be a virgin. Ashantis being matrilineal, the bride had to come from the maternal side of these particular homes – never from the paternal side. The Ama Ntosoa line, to which my mother belonged, was not one of these privileged homes. However, young women – from other homes – could be offered to the Ashanti king for marriage. Nana Akosua Kyem, being a big society lady of her time, had good contacts to the Ashanti king, Prempeh II, as well as to the queen mother (an important person in the society). Nana had wanted to give my mother to the king for marriage. However, my mother was not interested. Nevertheless, this would have been enforced if she had not gone to Achimota College.

Mama was a child of the colonial times, and this meant the beginning of the new age with its westernised influences that were fascinating for an educated young girl of her time. She understood her culture and was aware of the benefits, demands, and restrictions associated with this privileged marriage. It meant a life of isolation in the compound-courtyard of the Asantehene. His wives were never free to leave the compounds without special permission. A rare visit to a sick mother was allowed, and the Asantehene's wife would be escorted by some of her personal servants as well as by specially trained guards, who led the whole way proclaiming – out loud – that the Asantehene's wife was approaching and all men had to vanish or turn their backs to the on coming entourage. These guards were eunuchs, so they could not have any sensual activities with the bored wives. They were usually referred to as Asantehene's "elephants" because they were so fat.

My mother grew up at the time when formal education was instituted in Ashanti. She entered school and soon exhibited an aptitude for learning. Mama loved reading, which exposed her to the western world. She was fascinated by this world. Later, she received a scholarship that enabled her to attend the prestigious

Achimota Teacher Training College near Accra. She did not graduate because she met my father in the company of a cousin, who was dating a European. Shortly after that, he proposed to marry her, and she accepted.

As Ashantis have a matrilineal system, the oldest male on Nana Akosua Kyem's side of the family had to give my mother's hand in marriage. This was Nana's older brother, James Yaw Adjayekyem. He was highly respected as head of the extended family and as a paterfamilias. In addition to his own children, he also educated his sister's children. He was affectionately know by all and sundry as "Papa". He was very fair and treated his own children and his nephews and nieces alike. He was also skilful at mediating disputes between family members. Papa was the one my father approached. After all the relevant native ceremonies were performed, he accepted Charles Albert Brunner into the family.

A few centuries before, this would not have happened. Those days, Ashanti women never married outside the tribe. They had the responsibility of keeping the lineage purely Ashanti. To do otherwise was a scandal for the family. The lineage would be stained forever, and no one from this lineage would ever be chosen to be a chief. This is because a chief had to have a 100 percent Ashanti blood. This tradition led to inbreeding. Over time, it was realised that it was healthy to intermarry, and it led to intermarriages with other tribes and even slaves. My maternal great-grandfather, Nana Kwame Kyem, Bantamahene, is said to have later on in life taken a slave girl – from the northern region of Ghana – as a wife, a decision that scandalised Ashanti upper class society at the time.

I was born two months after my father died. My brother Maurice was twenty months old, and Charles was six and a half years old at the time. Growing up with our stepfather, John Knuckey, and our two half sisters, Brenda and Caroline, I saw my mother as a contented and harmonious person, at peace with herself and her surroundings. She seemed happy and felt privileged to have been able after my Swiss father's death to marry another European – especially an Englishman from colonial ruler, England. She enjoyed the status this afforded her in the Ashanti culture.

Mama was the traditional woman devoted to her family, and all her children were living with her under one roof. She was very grateful for this fact and never forgot it. She felt her position provided the best opportunities for all her five children.

In those days, Europeans would choose to marry Ghanaian women only if the woman had no children. It was then common for the prospective bride to fabricate lies about any children she may have had before with an African, claiming them to be her siblings or nephews and nieces. Sometimes, the man knew that she had children and would marry her but demand that her children live with relatives at his expense, and that would be the arrangement. To some Ghanaian women, it was advantageous to marry Europeans because of the material benefits and elevated social status. The ruling class was, after all, European. Still today, for many Ghanaians, white-skinned people stand for wealth and luxury.

I look back at my mother today as a pragmatist. She loved her children, and she was proud of them. Her objective was to keep us all together. My mother saw my independent ways as being different from hers and would often remark, "Annette should have been a boy". I think she admired me. She saw me as strong and sensible, and she confided much in me. During our many conversations, she emphasized that I should aim for a profession before marriage because financial dependence on a husband tends to make him too dominant. She also mentioned marriage is difficult, but I should try and avoid a divorce because it hurts to see your child hurting at the hands of a step-parent.

I loved my mother. She was for me an Ashanti lady. Like most children, I learned from my mother's actions and inactions in life. She did the best with the opportunities given her during her time. Women at the time accepted to be homemakers, devoting themselves solely to their families, as compared to now, when women want to be more in control of their lives.

She died in 1999 in London of cancer of the pancreas. A Ghanaian doctor in Accra had a year earlier diagnosed her with liver cancer. Doctors in the UK ran other tests and proclaimed her healthy. They missed completely any signs of the cancer that took her life. After months of being clueless as to the cause of her stomach pain, they finally opened her up and discovered the pancreatic cancer. The cancer was too far advanced for them to begin any treatment. They made her comfortable to await the inevitable. Although we all knew it was coming, her death was painful for all of us. She told us to bury her in London and that every ground is part of this earth. This was in contrast to the traditions of the Ashantis in which people of good lineage were expected to be buried in Ashanti soil. Her wish for a simple burial was fulfilled. A small funeral service was organized in London for just family and friends who could make it. All her five children, John, and Charlie's daughter Angela, whom she had raised because Angela's mother died giving birth to her, attended this funeral.

John also died two years later in England of cancer. He was cremated and buried next to his wife. Maurice, Brenda, and Angela represented our family at his funeral and burial.

My siblings – living in Kumasi.

My Biracial Siblings

My mother had three children with her first husband, Carl Albert Brunner. The eldest is Charles, followed by Maurice. I was the last born. Charles and I did not often fraternize because he was nearly seven years older than me. Because Maurice was about two years older than me, we played often together. I copied what he did. I was a tom boy. I never really enjoyed playing with dolls. My two brothers went to St Augustine Secondary School in Cape Coast. Charles went on to the University of Ghana in Accra at Legon. Maurice won a scholarship to study engineering at the Swiss Federal Institute of Technology in Zurich, known popularly by its Swiss acronym ETH. It was here that he completed his doctorate in civil engineering.

Brenda and Caroline (known as Carol) were the Knuckeys. My mother's second husband was John Anthony Knuckey. Brenda is three years younger than me. Brenda and I attended St Louis Secondary School in Kumasi. Caroline was the last born. She was born four years after Brenda. She was a student at the Ghana International School in Accra. Brenda, Caroline, and I went on to the Queen's Secretarial College in London. Brenda studied International Law in Geneva years later.

Uncle George Boateng

George Boateng was my mother's only brother from the same mother. Their father, Nana Boateng, had other children with other women. As a chief, he was expected to have more than one wife. My uncle had fine features, was tall, dark, and handsome.

He called me "gypsy" because of the way my hair used to look. My feathery hair was often unkempt. He was called "Boat" by his friends. His nephews and nieces called him "Wofa [Uncle] Boateng". His mother and sisters called him, at times, "Boateng" and, at other times, "Kwabena" – his Ashanti day name.

Uncle Boateng had about eight children with his two wives. I had very little contact with them, for he and his family moved to Accra when I was very young. His two sisters – my mother and Maame Abena Asubonteng – stayed in Kumasi with their families. It was through visits to Nana Akosua Kyem, who stayed initially with Mama and later with Maame Asubonteng, that the two sisters' families frequently saw each other. As a result, we have remained in contact with each other to this day.

According to the grown-ups, Uncle Boateng's first wife allegedly had a quarrel with Nana and beat her up. It is possible that she gave Nana only a slap, but that was enough for Nana's family to be outraged. At that time, the woman and Uncle Boateng were either only married customarily or not yet married. Shortly after she "beat" up his mother, Uncle Boateng married her at the registrar's office. This was like a slap to his mother's face. In Ashanti, it is unacceptable to beat up your father- or mother-in-law. Normally, you would be fined very heavily. Knowing how often her son was broke, Nana did not make a big case out of it. However, Nana never talked to her daughter-in-law again. Neither did most of the relatives. Nana felt betrayed by her only son's behaviour. Among other things, during World War II she had lied to protect him from being drafted into the British West African Colonial Army. The family had already lost Auntie Sophia's brother (Kwaku Afriyie – the Hercules and protector of relatives when in trouble) in Burma and were not willing to make another sacrifice in places none of them had ever heard of or even cared about. Boateng was her only son, and Nana spoilt him and was very hurt by his behaviour at this time and later.

Uncle Boateng was a building contractor. Although educated, he was obsessed about juju and witchcraft. When he began making money, he started going to juju men to supposedly protect himself against witchcraft. These juju men, sensing easy prey, hovered over him like vampires and bled him for all they could get. He even took little interest in his work, leaving it in the hands of unreliable people while he toured Europe with his wives, especially Number Two, who could neither read nor write. There were rumours that Number Two had put a spell on him, and judging from how besotted he was with her, you could be forgiven for believing it. He was an excellent father to Yvonne, his only child with Number Two, but, he neglected his children from his first marriage.

His new gurus came to spy the land and told him that his mother was a witch and was to blame for his difficulties, which, to any impartial observer, were of his own doing. Later, another juju man came to spy on Mama and also quickly concluded that she was a witch. His second wife believed this rubbish and maybe even encouraged it. It kept him occupied so he would not notice her many infidelities. Unfortunately, Maame Asubonteng also believed this superstitious nonsense. So it was poetic justice in a way, when yet another juju man later identified her as an even bigger witch, who had been operating in the shadow of her mother and sister. Auntie Sophia was also added to Uncle Boateng's pantheon of family witches. It sounds incredible and even hilarious, but true.

Uncle Boateng's attitude was bizarre to say the least. His sisters were always there for him. He liked the good things in life, but in his youth he could not afford them. Whenever he needed financial help, and that was often, he always turned to his sisters. Even later when he became rich, whenever things got tough for him, it was to his much-maligned sisters he turned for financial assistance and they always helped him. He rarely paid them back.

As a child, I was known to be a very deep sleeper. Waking me up was a difficult task. I recall rare visits of Uncle Boateng to our home. When my mother would announce he was going to sleep over, it always filled me with apprehension. Uncle Boateng could snore. The house seemed to shake as his snores reverberated through the whole house, all night long. Sleeping was impossible.

Wofa Boateng had a stroke at a relatively young age and suffered abominably for many years from its effects. He passed away still relatively young.

Maame Abena Asubonteng

My auntie, Maame Abena Asubonteng, was my mother's half sister. She was tall and had light-brown skin and fine features. She spent all her life in Kumasi. She married twice and had eleven children. Her own children called her "Maame", which means "mother". All other children, including relatives, called her "Maame", which, although spelt in the same way, is pronounced differently and is a title of respect meaning "Madam". All grown-ups called her, "Abena" – her Ashanti day name.

Maame Abena Asubonteng was the oldest child and the real business woman of all Nana's children. She never went to school, which makes her success in business all the more remarkable. When Nana's second marriage to Nana Akwasi Nkore of Patase ended, she moved back to Kumasi with her three children. Nana was used to living in the relative luxury of her father's court in Kumasi, so her husband's more modest house and lower standard of living in the village of Patase was a comedown, which Nana with her sharp tongue, I am sure, never ceased to remind him during their quarrels. According to Mama, he used to beat Nana. Considering how Nana could dress people down with her sharp tongue, I am not surprised that the normally calm Nana Akwasi Nkore was driven to get physical with her sometimes. In those days, it was a man's right to discipline a woman with his fists.

Although Nana came from Patase, she spent most of her life in Kumasi. Her brother, James Yaw Adjeikyem, who was educated, decided to put his nephew and nieces through school. Ashantis had finally come around to accept that it was a good idea to educate girls. My mother and her brother adapted easily to school life. Their big sister, Abena Asubonteng, did not. She was much older than her classmates and could not stand the teasing and the sadistic caning. She, therefore, dropped out.

Maame first went to work with her mother, Nana, trading and sometimes selling roasted yams and plantains. When she came of age, Nana gave her seed money to start her own business. She was privileged to have her own shop, which was located between the market and the shopping centre. It was a well located shop in a block of buildings that faced the street in the centre of Kumasi.

This auntie was reserved and serious. I recall her speaking mainly to the grown-ups. She was practical and had a realistic outlook about life. I have always respected her for raising all her children as a working mother. Maame never wore a dress in her life. She was a traditional woman and always wore the Ashanti attire – *kaba* and two pieces of cloth as wraps with a matching head kerchief. She attended funerals regularly as part of her social responsibilities in Kumasi.

Maame Asubonteng was a convert to Anglicanism and went to church every Sunday. I am told one day she was visited by Maame Apoaa. For some inexplicable reason, this juju woman went into a trance during which her body shook violently and she started to whirl around as if possessed. Maame Asubonteng and her children panicked and started shouting "Jesus". The frenzied whirling stopped eventually, but they were shaken for days afterwards.

Maame is said to have died from complications related to diabetes.

Auntie Sophia Okpeke

Sophia Okpeke, was our favourite aunt. She was my mother's older first cousin. Unusual for her time, especially as a woman, she had basic school education. Being unable to have children of her own, she considered us as her children. I believe I was her favourite niece and the daughter she never had. I loved her. She was my second mother, and I found her very interesting.

Sophia or Afua Ammadea was how she was called by the grown-ups and Auntie Sophia by all of us children. Auntie Sophia was known for her good appetite. She ate every kind of meat and fish and threw nothing away. When a chicken was killed for a meal, practically every part of that chicken was eaten, including the head and feet.

She was tall, big, and strong. Her big, fat hands looked like boxing gloves. She also had big, fat feet. It was rumoured that she had once beaten two soldiers and had thrown them down some stairs. She was the amazon, the Bellona (the ancient Roman goddess of war) who took no nonsense when it came to defending her family.

Nana Akosua Kyem, who did not suffer fools gladly, often needed Auntie Sophia's support in her many verbal fights. When Nana lived in 0.1.108, Ashanti New Town, she was said to quarrel a lot with the landlord's wife. During those fights, a child was usually dispatched to fetch Auntie Sophia, the tigress, from the other end of town. One of the girls was also sent to the market to buy meat, because Auntie loved it. It was amazing how the landlord's wife, Maame Duku, shut up when Auntie was around. Auntie Sophia had a reputation throughout Kumasi for being a troublemaker. She was quarrelsome and could be violent. The alleged beating of some off-duty soldiers had enhanced her image. Maame Duku is said to have once come too close to Auntie Sophia, who tried to grab her. Fortunately, some of the male tenants who were listening in intervened and stopped Auntie. It was for the best, but it would have been nice for the family to see Auntie in action. What people can remember is the look of fear in Maame Duku's eyes. Once, Auntie actually managed to grab her opponent and shook her, but quick action by the neighbours once again stopped Auntie from beating her up. Fortunately, nobody there knew that even by touching her, Auntie had committed technical assault. Maame Duku was said to be a real bitch and was not popular with the other tenants. These quarrels could go on for the better part of the day and provided entertainment for bored neighbours and for the children. Twi is a very earthy language, and the profanities the women used would have made a missionary's ears curl up with embarrassment. It had always been drummed into us children not to use such words, so Charles, who was sometimes around, said the children were shocked and, at the same time, fascinated to hear the grown-ups using such strong language. He and our older cousins would have something to gossip about for days on end. They would also practise using those awful words. The landlord eventually tried to evict Nana, but she took him to court and won her case. Charles remembers that very day very clearly. Nana dressed in white and covered her face and hands with a locally made white powder called "hyire" (pronounced "shiray"), a traditional way of celebrating victory.

Auntie Sophia was an emancipated woman at a time when it was customary for women to bow before men. In times of trouble, which were many, she was the family's protector and good to have around. At peaceful times, with no outside threats, she could be difficult and quarrelsome within her family. She was also feared by children because of her robust and rough ways, but her gruff manner and fearsome reputation hid a kind and generous soul. I was said to be the only one not afraid of her and could stand up to her.

One day, she was raving and ranting and being her usual self. No one dared stand up to her. I was about four years old. I remember standing up, facing her, shrugging my shoulders, and saying, "Just let me be. That is why you are the only one on this earth who can remove all your teeth".

She wore dentures. Being small, I did not realise I had touched a very sensitive subject. However, it worked, for it kept her quiet for a couple of days. She knew she was the topic of the restrained giggling among the family members.

This was a time in Ghana when there were very few dentists. Besides, most people could not afford to go to a dentist. It was, therefore, common to seek services from the local medicine man for dental problems. A dark, herbal, medicinal preparation was packed around the aching tooth. Within a short time, not only did one painlessly lose the problem tooth, but also lost a couple of healthy neighbouring teeth along with it. Sometimes, a whole row of teeth was lost. The few

European trained dentists seemed to also be more interested in removing teeth rather than fixing them. As a result, many people lived with few teeth in their mouths. Auntie Sophia was, however, one of the privileged few to be able to afford dentures. She was a business woman who sold cloth in those days.

Somehow, she admired my forthright ways. Perhaps, she saw herself in me. She would often take me into her arms, hugging and squeezing me. She made me feel special and loved, and I knew she would always stand by me.

World War II brought about the need for more men to fight on the side of the Allies. So, African men were recruited. Ghana, then known as the Gold Coast, is said to have lost 40,000 soldiers on the side of the Allies. Auntie Sophia's only brother, Kwaku Afriyie, is said to be among these soldiers that died. He joined the army for adventure.

It is interesting to note that before the war, the British preferred to recruit men from the northern region of Ghana because they were reputed to be stronger, more hard working, and more obedient than those of the other tribes – in particular, the Ashantis. This is because people from the northern region have a patrilineal system. Therefore, from a young age they went to farms with their fathers and helped them with the back-breaking jobs. This made them very strong. Being with men they got shouted at a lot, so they took more easily to life in the army. Also coming from a poorer part of the country they were motivated not to rock the boat.

On the other hand, from a young age, Ashantis spent more time with their womenfolk who were gentler. Ashanti recruits, therefore, resented being shouted at for seemingly no apparent reason. Often they shouted right back at the NCO or officer, thus earning them a reputation for insubordination. Another bone of contention was the work. Ashantis felt work such as cleaning toilets, kitchens, and other menial tasks was beneath them. They were used to seeing northerners and other domestic migrants doing such work. So they sometimes refused to do such work and, hence, their reputation for being lazy.

Interestingly, many Europeans also feel the same way about doing such work, which is done mainly by foreigners in Europe. However, when Europeans go into the army, they do not expect foreigners to do such jobs for them.

Thus, it took quite a while for it to sink into the heads of Ashantis that the army was an enclosed community and that they had to do everything themselves. Once they understood, they took to life in the army, and today many Ashantis are serving in the army.

Despite these problems, Ashantis are very good warriors. After all, they resisted the British in many battles and were the overlords of what later became known as Ghana.

Kwaku Afriyie, believing his chances of being recruited as an Ashanti was remote, gave himself the northern Ghanaian name of Mamadu Wangara. As the war progressed, the British in the Gold Coast instituted a draft for all young men eighteen and older. If he had waited a short while he would have been drafted under his own name. Kwaku Afriyie is said to have protested about the bad treatment that they, the African soldiers, were getting and was beaten badly and died as a result of his injuries in Burma. Like other dead Africans, his body, was not sent home.

It is interesting the tricks people got up to avoid the draft. My uncle, George Boateng, simply moved to our ancestral village and spent most of the time hiding in the farms. His mother, Nana, claimed he was dead. A colleague of his was not so lucky, but he outwitted the British authorities. He was asked to bring his stool for inspection. He asked his mother to prepare okra soup, which he ate. His stool looked unhealthily green and slimy. The British military medics had never seen anything like it before. He was therefore discharged as being unfit to serve. They claimed he was harbouring an unknown disease.

Every culture has its fairy tales or stories. Storytelling is necessary in each culture to help explain life in an attempt to guide children into the society in which they find themselves and finally into adulthood. The stories explain what is expected socially with regard to behaviours, attitudes, principles, and morals.

In Ashanti folklore, there is a character, Kwaku Anansi (literally Kwaku the Spider) who is the villain in all folk stories. Auntie Sophia told us many of these stories. She, a proud Ashanti, was anxious about instilling Ashanti culture in us children.

She also gave us Ashanti day names, Kofi for Charles, Yaw for Maurice, Afua for Annette, Yaa for Brenda and Akua for Carol. Unfortunately, the names did not catch on. Our other relatives refused to call us by anything other than our given names. As was true with all our Ashanti relatives, we communicated in Twi.

Auntie Sophia lived in one of the many government-constructed housing developments in South Suntreso, near Bantama, Kumasi. She bought the house herself. It was a cheaply built, semi-detached, small house with a fenced-in courtyard. The amenities were basic. It had one bedroom and a living room. It had a pantry, which also served as a kitchen when it rained. Cooking was normally done in the small courtyard. Also within the courtyard, but separated from the house, was a bathroom and a separate latrine – both with untiled walls.

The house was built below street level! Added to this was poor drainage. Each tropical rain turned her neighbourhood into a flooded zone. So were the inside of the houses. In order to remedy this problem, a high concrete wall of at least one metre was constructed in front of the door, facing the street to keep the water out of the house. The structure was not very attractive, but it served the purpose.

Auntie Sophia, like most women of her generation, dressed in cloth with the *kaba* top, in the Ashanti traditional manner. These printed cloths were imported from England and Holland. Men also dressed in these cloths, which could measure four metres long. They wore them like togas – Roman style.

My sister Brenda and I spent two days with her during a mid-term break. With her permission, we went to see the six o'clock movie, at the Rivoli, in her neighbourhood, one night. We bought tickets for the front-row seats. They were the cheapest. After the first movie, we decided to stay for the second feature. Our necks ached because our seats were so close to the screen, but we were having fun.

Our fun was short lived once the film ended. It was late, way past our scheduled return home. We were overcome by a dreadful feeling of fear. In silence we started unhurriedly towards Auntie Sophia's house. No one spoke. The nearer we drew to the house, the harder my heart pounded. As we approached the house's entrance, my sister silently took her position behind me. I was older. Suddenly, we heard loud voices from the living room. Sophia and Bob, her husband, were quarrelling over us.

We heard Bob yell, "When they go and do their thing, then they say I did it!"

We were shocked. My sister was twelve and I was fifteen, and we were innocent. Besides, we had never accused him of anything.

Auntie yelled back, "Bob, if you are a man, dare repeat what you just said!"

He dared and repeated what he had said. By this time, we were standing in the doorway, in a state of shock, as we witnessed them physically fighting over us. Auntie Sophia stood six feet tall. Her husband, a Nigerian, stood more than six feet tall. He was well built. Suddenly in a swift movement, we saw Auntie Sophia grab her husband's Bermuda shorts and yank them down, baring his buttocks. Having thus immobilised him, she quickly bent him over her ample thighs, where she proceeded to spank him.

He managed to break loose, ran into his bedroom shouting in pidgin English, "I *taya* oooohhh, I *taya* oooohhhhh!" (meaning, "I am fed up").

Always the one to have the last word, Auntie quipped back, "You *taya*? You *taya*? Do you think marriage is easy?"

During our years at St Louis Secondary School, Auntie Sophia would sometimes visit us on Sundays. Receiving visitors was always special because the school was located in an isolated area, outside Kumasi, and students were not allowed to leave the school grounds. Visitors never came empty handed and neither did Auntie Sophia.

Upon her arrival at the school, she would set out looking for Brenda and me in the different dormitories. In the meantime, half the school would also be in search of us. In no time, at all, we would hurriedly make our way to welcome and embrace her. I would have my close friends by, knowing she would bring food for us. We knew it would take a while before we could start eating the meal because Auntie Sophia was a staunch Christian, a member of the Pentecostal Church. She prayed before meals. More accurately, I should say, she gave a sermon. The prayer would start with thanksgiving and continue with the seeking of blessings, covering all aspects of our lives. At long last, we would arrive at the "Amen" and heave a sigh of relief.

Auntie Sophia was a good cook. Her *fufu* was delicious and remarkably warm. We would sit in a circle with the food in the middle and eat with our right hands.

I look back and admire this woman for the great efforts she made to come and visit us. It probably took her all morning to prepare the food. She depended on very poor public transportation to make it to our school and then return home.

Auntie Sophia died in 1998 at the age of ninety from natural causes.

Cousin Cicero Oduro

Cicero Oduro was our favourite cousin. His mother was Maame Asubonteng. His Ashanti name was Kwadwo Kwateng. Cicero was full of life, bubbling with energy and ideas. He sucked in anything he found interesting and useful for his life in Ashtown (the short form of Ashanti New Town), Kumasi. He was often misunderstood at home because of his personality. In Ashanti culture, he was regarded as someone who rocked the boat. He had a questioning mind and was curious and accepting of different cultures. He was always ready to learn and try new ways.

Kwateng often came to our house to play with my brother, Maurice, who was of the same age. He noticed how we children would kiss and hug our mother many times a day. Showing open affection the way we did with our mother was not the norm in Ashanti culture. Kwateng liked what he saw. So, when he got home, he would walk straight to his mother and start hugging and kissing her – just like we did. He did this in front of everyone – in a compound setting! His mother loved his spontaneous ways, but she felt she had to protest each time because it was not natural in Ashanti culture.

CiiCii, as he was called by friends, pointed out to me years later that even our food was different. How, I wondered? I thought it was the same type of Ashanti soups that my Ashanti mother prepared! No, he corrected me. It was good and very different. What made it so different from other groundnut, palm nut, and light soups? Yes, now I know. My mother, a housewife, often left out many of the ingredients, such as the stink fish (dried fish), that gave the real Ashanti soups that very special and authentic flavour. It also had little pepper, making it easy for us children to consume. This is because my mother, like her mother, Nana, did not like spicy foods. John, our stepfather, sometimes liked to try the soups but could not stand spicy foods. He also despised stink fish. It made him want to throw up. This reminds me of a few stories not directly related to CiiCii.

One day, Mama decided to prepare cocoyam-leaf stew flavoured with stink fish in the courtyard, away from the kitchen and the rest of the house. In no time at all, the fish made its presence felt. As the stink wafted through the house, John appeared on the back veranda and told Mama to throw it away. He could not imagine how any one could possibly want to eat such smelly fish. Mama retorted that he also ate smelly cheeses that we found disgusting too. In a huff, he went to the beer bar next door. When he came back, the food was ready, and he actually tried it and said it was not bad at all.

Mama believed her soups with the stink fish did not stink. She had smelt worse soups before. Before John came into our lives, Mama had a tenant, Adja Yaw, an Ewe, a herbalist, and juju man who lived in the basement. I don't know what ingredients he put in his soup, but it used to really stink. One day while he was cooking, the smell was so strong that Nana felt compelled to confront him, so she went into the basement. Adja Yao was outraged that anybody would find his soup smelly.

He took the pot off the fire and shoved it under Nana's nose, so she got a really good whiff, repeatedly asking her, "Does this stink?"

For once, Nana was speechless; then she beat a hasty retreat to take in oxygen outside. She said the smell stayed with her for several weeks. Adja Yao was evicted before John moved in with us. Mama wanted to spare his civilized English nostrils the unforgettable experience of smelling Adja Yao's malodorously aromatic soups wafting through the house. Adja Yao was an irascible old man, and although younger, Nana was almost as cranky. It was always interesting whenever they squared off over some transgression on his part. Mostly Nana came on top, but occasionally, he scored a point.

CiiCii's comments reminded me about how my mother, a housewife, took time to cook agreeable meals for her children. Children were very much loved and valued in Ashanti culture. This same culture, however, forced a child to eat exactly what the grown-ups ate. The food was often too spicy for the little ones. One has to acquire certain tastes with time. However, most mothers had to work all day. When they got home in the evenings, supper had to be ready before dusk. So, there was no time to prepare separate meals for the children.

Our mother broke certain Ashanti norms to protect her children. Those days, Ashantis used hot pepper and ginger not only in their meals but also medicinally. Ground pepper and ginger were also put in the private parts to cure infections. My grandmother went as far as using them as ear drops for ear infections. In Ashanti, naughty children were disciplined in many ways, some of them, I am told, horrendously. One of the worst was having freshly ground pepper or ginger or a combination of the two inserted into your rectum if you were a boy or into both the rectum and the vagina if you were a girl. One can only too well imagine how very painful this must have felt. Charles said it was done to him too, and he swears to this day, it was a barbaric and inhumane punishment. He tells me Mama put a stop to it when it was about to be done to me, and as she was the moneybags at the time, they stopped. It was probably done to Mama, too, when she was young.

Growing up in Kumasi

A home for the average Ashanti at the time was a rented room or two in a compound house. Furnishing for the rooms was sparse. It usually consisted of a metal bed – imported from England – for the adults. Wooden beds were really not in vogue among the Ashantis at the time. The children slept on the floor on bare woven straw mats.

All tenants shared one untiled bathroom with no water outlet. So, for bathing, a bucket of water had to be carried each time into the bathroom. Often, only one toilet, a bucket latrine, was available for all tenants, and so, the public latrines in the neighbourhood were frequently used. These latrines were known locally as "bombers". These were squatting compartments without doors. The toilets were holes in the concrete floors with a bucket latrine underneath each hole that was emptied sporadically. Gasses therefore built up in the buckets. Occasionally, a smoker would drop a lit cigarette butt into the bucket. There would be an unpleasant explosion, hence, the name "bombers". Imagine the embarrassment of telling people your father, brother, or husband died in such a manner.

Our family home in Kumasi was in a new developing residential area, near Krofofrom (in English it means a new township). There was a road in front of our house. Our house was surrounded by empty plots of land covered with thick bushes. We had a big garden with mango, avocado, banana, and orange trees, the fruits of which we enjoyed in season. Nearby was a forest reserve. As a result, our constant unwelcome visitors were lizards and the various snakes of the tropics, including the dreaded black cobra and the green mamba. We were instructed to give the snakes a wide berth and not provoke them.

Our house was built of cement blocks with a flat concrete roof and was considered big. It was set on relatively large grounds surrounded by red hibiscus hedges. It had three bedrooms, a veranda in front of the living room, which faced the street, and another veranda, which faced the garden and back yard. There was a sparsely furnished kitchen with a gas stove and a built-in sink and cupboards. Next to the kitchen was our dining room with a very large wooden table and wooden chairs for our family of seven.

When we grew up with John, he introduced us to certain British norms. We had to eat together at table. Each one had his or her own plate, cutlery, and drinking glass. This was in sharp contrast to the Ashanti traditional way of eating from a common bowl with our right hands. Traditionally, locals used the calabash or tinned mugs for drinking. The calabash is made when the inside of the gourd is scoured out and the outer hard shell is dried and used as a drinking bowl. Nowadays, locals use tin or plastic mugs for drinking. In more sophisticated homes, people use plates, cutlery, and glasses and likewise in the secondary schools and universities.

Our home was sparsely furnished. We had wooden beds, wardrobes, and cupboards in the bedrooms. These beds had imported mattresses and pillows. The bottom and top sheets over the mattresses were white. A thin blanket over the sheets, tucked in neatly on the sides, was enough to keep us warm. The living room had African styled wooden chairs with cushions and side tables for each chair. We had a centre table. One never bought furniture from a shop. Furniture was always ordered from the many carpentry shops around. We had linoleum on the floor. All windows had screens to help ward off mosquitoes. Behind the mosquito net was a wire netting (outside the window) to keep thieves at bay. The doors had metal bars, placed horizontally from the inside, each night, to make it impossible for anyone to easily force it open from the outside. This was the basic security measure taken in those days. It was, however, very effective for we never had a burglary.

Initially, we also used the bucket latrines that were in vogue until the late fifties. There was a bathroom, that was not tiled and neither was the toilet. Later, this was remodelled by John into a bathroom with a bath tub with a shower head and taps and white tiled walls. The floors had terrazzo tiles. The bucket latrine was then replaced by a water closet connected to a septic tank that got emptied regularly.

It was normal for relatives to live with the owner of the house, but John wanted proper servants, who knew what they were doing. Native male servants were called "boys". We always had boys who cleaned the house, washed and ironed our clothes, and took care of the garden. The servants communicated with us in Twi and pidgin English, which is a sort of broken English spoken in West Africa by the uneducated. Nowadays the term "boy" is frowned upon in the West, but in Ghana, it still does not cause any offence. It is common to call male servants by this name, and the servants are not offended by it. There were also maids who were known by their own names. We had an old watchman and many dogs. We loved our dogs. Besides, they were a necessity for they were more alert to intruders. Most of our domestic helpers lived elsewhere, but after the day's work, they took their baths behind our house with a bucket of water. They used the public latrines in the neighbourhood. They were given three meals in addition to a monthly salary.

My parents had friends from different nationalities and cultures. They were usually couples, and many had children. Socializing being an important part of life in Ghana, they visited us, and we in turn would visit them, especially on Sundays. At these get-togethers, one noticed how the different nationalities had different mannerisms. I noticed that the British were a bit more reserved than the continentals. The men drank lots of beer during these visits, and the children played together. We all spoke English with various accents.

Because many of the people present were Europeans, European meals were served, except for special occasions, when chicken groundnut soup of the Ashanti region was served with rice and *fufu*. Sometimes, chicken curry, prepared the Ghanaian way, was also served with rice. For some reason Europeans did not like palm soup, which with our African palates we enjoyed. Ground hot pepper was usually set separately at the table for those who had acquired the tropical taste of hot, spicy meals. Boiled, cooled water was always served at meal times for all – including the beer-drinking men.

Looking back, I recall how the Europeans talked more to us children than to the African women present at these gatherings. This made me somehow feel accepted by them. I sensed recognition. I felt equal to them. However, my mother often made side comments such as, "We're just overlooked", referring to the African women present. As a child, I of course, never gave this much thought.

As an adult, I was to fully assess and understand the world in which I grew up in. Most of the white men at such gatherings had Ghanaian wives or girlfriends and did not want to cause offence by talking intimately to someone's wife or girlfriend. It was safer to talk to the children. Truth be told, the African women were also reserved with the European men. Having suffered under the colour bar of the colonial times, they were still reticent around white people, especially white women. My mother, having grown up during this era, had also been scarred. It took her many years to overcome her discomfit. When she got to know white people better, she realised that they were just people whose skins are white. I also learnt from my many travels that the European sense of white supremacy (before independence) and the sense of inferiority inflicted on the African were also common in many parts of the world where Europeans met other races, irrespective of colour.

Parental care in Kumasi, at the time, was very loose when both parents worked. Parents provided very little supervision, but informal supervision was provided in the community by relatives, neighbours, and friends. Most children, therefore, led a free life of little supervision. Our stepfather insisted that our mother should be a stay-at-home mom. As a result, we (her children) had a lot of care and protection.

A well brought up child from the Ashanti tribe was taught not to look directly into the eyes of grown-ups when addressed. One often avoided eye contact as a sign of respect. On the other hand, in the western world, it is seen as impolite when one avoids eye contact during conversations. John insisted that we should look people in the eye when being addressed. So, my brother Maurice and I looked directly into people's eyes, and we were excused and accepted. People often found our affable, forthright, and impulsive ways amusing. We were happy, busy children, naturally curious and interested in our world and the people around us. We were always getting ourselves into awkward situations with our impulsive behaviours. This caused our grandmother much embarrassment.

There are many stories of our impulsive ways when we were very young. We were said to stare rudely at people who were physically challenged in any way. Why they looked different was of great interest to us. However, Ashanti culture did not encourage children to ask offensive questions, so very little was explained to us. Children were meant to be seen, not heard. We were always told to shut up, whenever we asked questions. This was partly because the adults did not know the answers and felt too proud to own up to ignorance about something to a child. But that did not stop us. What did we do? We would simply go to the disabled person and ask them why they were different. It caused a lot of embarrassment for them and the grown-ups around. We, of course, never noticed the uncomfortable state we had created. We were so involved in trying to find answers.

Finally, our grandmother decided enough was enough. These people should not be subjected to endless questioning about their conditions each time they paid us a visit. So, she elicited the help of our mother to talk to us, for we could not go on like that. We were causing too much embarrassment. Our mother sat down with us and gently explained the situation to us, convincing us not to ask any more questions. We could look but we were to say nothing. We promised to do so. Shortly after came our next victim. She was going from house to house trying to sell her wares.

Nana gave us a meaningful look, "Remember what your mother said!!!"

Well, we looked. This was a most interesting case. The woman had a big protuberance around her neck, almost the size of a small ball. We checked our natural impulse to ask questions that would hurt her. We remembered what our mother had managed to convey to us. No, we did not want to hurt her, but she sure had an interesting condition! I leaned on the stairs so I could get a better look at the poor woman who had been offered a stool, by our grandmother, while she went inside to fetch our mother. I said nothing, like I had been told. My brother, Maurice, also said nothing. There was silence. Suddenly, he grabbed a stool and placed it right in front of her, sat down, so he could studiously assess her head and neck – like a scientist doing research.

Nana took in the scene from the corner of her eye, at the top of the stairs. She burst into the room where our mother was and cried with dismay and despair and told our mother her children were up to their usual tricks again. Our mother glanced down at us from a window and called us to come in. We went inside and she told us to wait for her. In the meantime, she went out to the woman and bought some of the wares she was selling. This was to make up for our rude stares. The woman, with the bulge on her neck, never set foot in our home again. In fact, she is said to have always taken a detour around our house when she was in the neighbourhood.

Our parents being often away and we finding ourselves alone with our grandmother, Maurice and I would often resort to playing tricks on her in order to get our way. She had her instructions from our mother. Once we wanted to go to the movies but knew she would not permit us to go because it was, in her opinion, too late. Maurice and I decided he would wait in the forest reserve across our house for me. This was on the way to the Odeon cinema, which was about a mile from our home. I would go home and ask: "Nana, Nana, where is Maurice?" Upon replying she did not know where he was, I would reply, "I'll go and look for him". I would then join Maurice, and we would go to the movies. The thought of the stress we were causing this poor old woman never crossed our minds. I was about eight and Maurice was barely ten.

When the time came to put our plan into action, I developed cold feet. I could not lie to my Nana. My eyes would betray me, I thought. No. Maurice was to do this. After all, he was the man, and he was older. I knew it was just as difficult for him, but I had him in a corner. I had challenged his manhood, and he had to deliver.

I waited and waited. I heard the sounds of the various animals and insects in the woods. Where on earth was he? Dusk, very short in the tropics, was approaching and with it the dark night with its thousand eyes and sounds. There I was alone in the forest. My heart throbbed with anxiety. I was afraid. After what seemed like a lifetime, my brother appeared running as fast as he could. He was a good runner. I admired his speed for he had beaten me in racing on many occasions.

"Hurry, hurry, you must run fast. We'll be late for the movie!" he panted as he whizzed past me.

I tried to catch up with him. I wanted to know why he took so long. He then told me between breaths, as we ran, that he had also gotten cold feet and had had problems asking Nana the question. He had moved about the house and garden for a while, before he had had the courage to go through with our plan. This was one of the many reasons our grandmother would get worried and panicky about us.

That was, however, not going to stop us from going to the cinema. We just made it in time. We only had money for the cheapest seats. Our pocket money was never much. It was intended for sweets at the kiosk, which was run by a woman from the north of Ghana. We became totally absorbed in the film. Home was forgotten. Any concerns that we had created about our absence from home was also forgotten. Our worries started when the movie was over. Now, the thought of facing Nana filled us with apprehension. With heavy hearts and feet, we made our way home, anticipating the usual scene of our grandmother pacing up and down the street, in front of our house, sick with worry. Nana was so relieved to see us and thankful nothing had happened to her precious grandchildren, that she hugged us and tucked us in our beds.

Kejetia Market, Kumasi

A stall at Kejetia Market.

Kejetia Market, Kumasi

One cannot talk about life in Kumasi without mentioning Kejetia market. Attending St Bernadette Catholic Primary School as day pupils, we were required to attend Sunday Mass. The Roman Catholic Church was on the hill overlooking Kejetia market, and so I had to traverse the market to and from church. I usually went in the company of an older relative.

Life in the open-air market at Kejetia, Kumasi, was always interesting. The market was said to be one of the largest such markets in West Africa. It was right in the centre of town. It consisted of many stalls, lined up in rows, with rusty tin roofs. There were also little shops, which were rickety constructions with the usual tin roofs. The roofs were a necessary protection from the heavy rains and blazing sun.

The market was lively, loud, busy, and dusty. There were small heaps and piles of litter here and there. People hawked their goods at every turn. There was a strong mixture of smells in the humid air. There was the pungent smell of dried fish and dried meat, the sweet sickly smell of the blood of freshly slaughtered animals, the smell of rotting vegetables and foodstuffs, and the strong body odour of people doing heavy manual work. The climate was not only stuffy from the hot humidity, but the place was intriguing – to say the least. The atmosphere was always changing, and there was always mayhem.

There was loud shouting as people went about their daily

business advertising their wares at the top of their voices. Due to the hustle and bustle, there were also the occasional fights when someone upset the wares of a vendor. Every so often, the din of noise would escalate into a deafening uproar. Some petty thief had just been seen stealing and had regrettably got away. There is a general Ghanaian custom of beating thieves when they are caught. In extreme cases, some are even murdered.

I doubt if vehicles without horns could be driven through Kejetia market. Cars, buses, trucks, and *trotros* were constantly honking at pedestrians and animals for the same space. Trotros are small buses or trucks that are used to transport passengers. You could not hurry for it was packed with people, some selling or buying and most trying to move from one point to another. One just moved along with the thick, sweaty, noisy crowd.

The market offered all the food products of the region, including yams, which are a staple food in Ghana. It was easy to find imported goods like pomades for the body and hair and all kinds of soap. Meat was often sold on wooden tables with no coolers. The livestock was usually slaughtered the very day of the sale, so the meat was always fresh. Flies were numerous and pervasive. Every now and then, a hand swipe would send them swarming around both sellers and buyers. Fresh fish was usually sold on ice blocks. Smoked fish was also available.

There were many shops in and around the open-air market in Kumasi. The shops outside the market were in concrete buildings and usually faced the street. They sold imported items from Europe, India, Hong Kong, and South Africa. There were products like clothing, shoes, radios, matches, tinned milk, sugar, corned beef, sardines, tomato puree, toffees, biscuits, powdered milk for babies and adults, and all things one needed for daily living.

Going to School in Ghana

The beginning of school for a child is an exciting and special time. Finally, you are old enough to start school! In the past, until about the late 1950s, children in Ghana started school at age six, but since most of the births were not registered, this age varied. Teachers assessed children for school entrance. To determine if they were of school age, they would have the child try to touch the opposite ear by reaching the arm over the top of the head – right arm to left ear or left arm to right ear. If you were able to perform this manoeuvre, you were ready for school.

A child attending a local primary school in Ghana then faced severe obstacles. There was no transportation for those who lived far from school. Timeliness for the student was a problem because few families possessed a clock. They usually gauged time by the position of the sun in the sky. Tardiness at school had dire consequences. You were caned heavily for being late without a good reason. Not having a clock or watch at home was *not* deemed to be a good reason.

Pupils were caned on the palms of the hands, on the buttocks, or on the back. Although parents valued education, few had ever seen the inside of a classroom. Consequently, there was no educational help at home. Teachers were well respected, and it was rare for a parent to side with a child against a teacher. Those days, teachers were pretty strict, and there was the occasional sadist.

I remember my brother Charlie telling us that once one of his classmates was severely beaten by the teacher over some trivial matter. The following day, the father of the pupil came to their classroom, and right in front of them all (needless to say, to their delight) beat the living day lights out of the teacher who had to be sent to the hospital. No charges were brought, because the head teacher realised that his own teacher could also be charged with assault.

An older cousin of mine was taken by my mother who was about sixteen at the time to be enrolled at the Government School in Kumasi. Below is a reconstruction of the interview:

Head teacher (HT): Do you speak Twi?

Pupil: Yes.

HT: Are you an Ashanti?

Pupil: No.

HT: How many eyes have you got?

Pupil: Four.

He was admitted, which means he did better than many others. He must have been very nervous to give such silly answers. Today he is a well educated, respected, and successful businessman. This goes to show that you can never tell, as Ashantis say, the beginnings of a great man.

Another cousin attended the Division Primary School near the Odeon Cinema in Kumasi. In those days, the teachers would cane you at the drop of a hat, so most pupils were always nervous. One morning he needed to use the bathroom, but he was afraid to tell the teacher and decided to hold on until the break. Unfortunately, his stomach had other ideas. And so it was that he did his business in his shorts right there in the classroom. As is normal in Africa, justice was swift and rough. He was marched out of the classroom to the school water taps, where he was made to strip naked and wash himself and his clothes without soap. A female relative, attending the same school, was summoned and made to give him her PE (physical education) shorts and blouse. The whole school knew they were cousins.

Thus it was that he suffered the shame of arriving home that afternoon in a girl's dress, carrying his reeking school uniform all wrapped up in a newspaper. This was a sadistic touch by the teachers. They could have given him soap to wash his clothes, but they did not because they wanted everyone to know what he had done. His female cousin would not talk to him for a long time. She felt he had disgraced her in public. They were both about eight years old. This was a very difficult thing to live down. The endless teasing by his classmates and the occasional teacher led this male cousin to start playing truant in a big way. He dropped out of school and started hanging out with a gang of thieves at Kumasi Zongo. His mother and Nana were very worried as were his siblings and playmates. Finally, his mother sent him to his father, who was the chief of Kyikyiwere, where he continued his education. Because of his stay at his father's court he was the only one left in the family well-versed in Ashanti court etiquette. He became a farmer in the Bari-Kesse area.

Charles recalls how this cousin, who was also his playmate

came home on one of his rare visits from Zongo. He had obviously not had a bath for a while. As we all know, in Africa, if you do not bath even for a day, everybody can smell you. Anyway, the other relatives who had to sleep next to him could not stand the stench any longer, so they boiled water, forcibly removed his cloth, and bathed him. This showed once again Africans' penchant for not too subtle behaviours.

Charles says he also played truant for a while, but his career as a truant was short lived. For reasons that he has since forgotten, the head teacher expressed a wish to see his mother. This was in class four. It had nothing to do with his academic work, because Charles was a good pupil. Anyway, Mama thought he wanted a bribe, a phenomenon that was beginning to rear its ugly head around that time, and she declined to meet him. Those were the days when the word or wish of the head teacher was law, and he did not take kindly to our mother's disinclination to see him. And so, Charles bore the brunt of his annoyance. He would single him out for abuse in the classroom and at assembly.

Charles became unhappy and started playing truant. He fell in with another classmate, a boy from the Ewe tribe, who felt the head teacher's sharp tongue even more. The Ewe had a real problem. For the first three years when the medium of instruction was Twi, he could barely keep up, because his mother tongue was Ewe, which is as different from Twi as English is from Russian. His teachers and peers regarded him, rather unfairly, as a dimwit. When English became the language of the class after class four, he was completely at sea. His parents were illiterate and could not help him. He needed special help instead of the constant caning and torrent of abuse he got. The head teacher, who taught them English, really went to town on him. This Ewe boy, therefore, started dodging classes, and Charles joined him.

One day, they went to where the Kumasi Museum is now, near Kumasi Central Hospital or Gee, as it is popularly known (after the British company that built it). At that time there was a growth of Para rubber trees in front of the library, behind which the museum stands. They used to collect the seeds to play a game called *nte* (in Twi). While they were searching in different parts of the growth but not far from one another, his fellow truant called Charles over to his side. He had just found a big cache. Charles had moved just about three yards, when he heard a sound like something heavy falling behind him. It was a huge green mamba that had fallen exactly where he had been standing just a few seconds earlier. Our country cousins had told him that the mamba was fond of taking swings at animals, including people, passing under a tree or just dropping on them and biting them. Charles was very lucky that day and took it as an omen. He never played truant again. He endured the verbal and physical abuse for a few more weeks before this sadistic head teacher got bored and left him in peace. This sadist had other poor souls to torment. The Ewe still continued and sadly dropped out of school not long afterwards.

The miracle was that children went to school at all. School was a place where many children were subjected to pain and humiliation. A pupil who failed to give a correct answer in class was not only caned but also subjected to a lot of insults and ridicule. Some simply just dropped out and stayed home to avoid such misery. Many, however, continued to show up at school.

Before private schools came onto the scene in Ghana, most elementary schools were run by missionaries or the government. As previously mentioned, the first three years of education were entirely in the local vernacular, but gradually, English superseded the local language. The books were then in English, and teachers communicated in English during classes. At home, however, Ghanaian languages were spoken. Those pupils from the villages had less exposure to English. So, school may have been the first time a child heard English being spoken. After our father's death, our mother is said to have grieved a lot. She became very depressed. In such a state, Nana and the servants took care of us children and so having non-educated people in charge, Twi became our language too.

Some children, however, came from homes where English was the primary language. These were normally homes where one of the parents was an English speaker. We were lucky in this sense because, when John moved in with our mother, we had to switch from speaking Twi to English at home, a situation which continues to today. This was so that John would not feel left out of conversations. This gave us a big advantage when we started school. Through John's influence and through contact with his European friends, we became not only fluent, but our accent also changed to be more British. Many educated Ghanaians spoke then and still speak

English to their children, so, they also have an advantage at school. As a result, as students entered secondary school, they exhibited a wide range of abilities in their knowledge of the English language. Some managed to master the language in the secondary schools, and some did not do so well.

Education during British colonial rule was for the privileged few because school fees had to be paid and not everyone could afford them. After independence in 1957, Kwame Nkrumah's socialist government made elementary school education compulsory but free for all children. Up to about the late 1950s, it took six years of primary school and four years of middle school to qualify for the secondary-school entrance examinations. Years later, it was possible to take the entrance exam after completing two years of middle school. Later, around 1961, after the introduction of international or preparatory schools, it was possible to enter secondary school after five years of primary school.

As Ghanaians became richer, they wanted better education for their children. There was an increase in demand for a better school system. Almost overnight, private primary schools started to spring up. Some were boarding schools. It seemed in those days you could not open a page of one of the local newspapers, *The Daily Graphic*, without reading about yet another new school opening its doors. Many of these private schools did not survive.

My Primary School Years

My first school, Our Lady of Assumption (OLA), was in Cape Coast. It was about 100 yards from the beach. It was a boarding school run by Roman Catholic nuns. It had an enrolment of not more than 100 children – if my memory serves me right. About half the pupils, like myself, were boarders, the rest were day pupils. I was about six years old. I was too young to be away from home, but that was life then. Parents saw it as a privilege to be able to send their children to the so-called good schools – at the time. These were schools modelled after British Public schools but were poorly run.

Our school was surrounded by thick walls, and it felt like being in prison. There was nothing to do after classes. It was so boring that sometimes I would climb about half way up a pillar, but all I could see outside was a huge grey ocean. Occasionally, I would see a few birds flying about. I envied them their freedom. There were no trees or vegetation whatsoever, and the compound was gravelled. Having grown up in a home with a large garden with trees and a forest reserve nearby, I found it desolate.

The European nuns in charge were reserved. After classes, we never saw them because they seemed busy praying. They left us in the care of lay people who bungled taking care of us. Ghanaians are, generally, warm people, but we were completely ignored by these people. It seemed we were just a number. No one seemed to really care for us.

My parents paid me a surprise visit to find me looking like a waif. All my belongings had been stolen. The only clothes I had left were the ones on my back. My hair had been shaven off because I had sores on my head. Under shock at my appearance and totally disappointed, my parents removed me from this school that very day. This was not the last time this would happen. I, however, returned home speaking Fanti fluently – the language of this area. Any trace of my fluent Twi – the language of the Ashantis – was erased. Fanti and Twi are the same language but spoken with very different accents. OLA is an educational institution. As such, the Fanti spoken there was in a clipped tone. I came back home speaking like that. My cousins, thereupon, nicknamed me "Awura Afua" (lady Afua) and at times, "Awura Annie" (lady Annie). A few months after my return, I lost the Fanti accent and again spoke Ashanti Twi. However, my nickname has remained to this day.

I was, of course, happy to be home in my normal environment close to my mother. For the first few months, I could not sleep at night. I would then tiptoe to my parent's bedroom where I would cuddle contentedly next to my mother, immediately falling asleep. The next morning, I would find myself in my own bed!

The next school was St Bernadette Catholic primary day school in Kumasi, close to home. It was run by Catholic nuns. One day, an Indian schoolmate invited me to go home with her after school to play. After she had reassured me she did not live far, I jumped into her car, and the driver drove us, without questioning, to her home. My grandmother, who was in charge of Maurice and me was, of course, not informed. Being of a very independent nature, I had made one of my many impulsive decisions without informing anyone.

Before dark, the Indian mother told me it was time to go home. I was shocked and looked at her for I had no idea where I was or which direction my home was. I guess this was not her problem, for she just took her daughter into the house and closed the door. I started walking and was petrified of the oncoming darkness. I plodded along, aimlessly. Night came, and it was pitch black. In the darkness of the night, I could not see my way. My senses were, however, very alert and I heard all kinds of sounds. Most of all I heard my heart pounding the loudest, tumm, tumm, tumm!!!

After what seemed like an eternity, I emerged from this total darkness onto a scene of several big open fires surrounded by people cooking. I continued at a slow pace, my eyes to the right, fixed on these people. Comics I had read, with drawings of men being cooked in similar large pots on open fires, crossed my mind. It all seemed so real. By this time, they had finally noticed my presence. From all corners people seemed to appear. They just kept on coming and took position behind the open fires, with their eyes fixed on me. More people converged from the darker sections of the compound, joining the gathered group. They seemed so numerous from a frightened seven-year-old's perspective. Those cooking stopped, their ladles held in mid-air. All other activities came to an abrupt halt. There was total silence. I was on one side of the fires, and they were on the other side. I kept my eyes on them, and they stared at me, wondering where I had come from, for it was clear I did not belong to this part of town. I was lighter skinned and obviously not part of their group.

Suddenly, a man came out of one of the quarters, saw the scene, and quickly walked towards me. He asked, "Are you lost?"

Frozen by fear and incapable of talking, (for the first time in my life – for I was a chatter-box), I nodded. He was an off-duty policeman. He told me he was from the Ewe tribe. At this, I froze. I had heard of tales of the people of the Ewe tribe kidnapping and cutting out the hearts of little children, for use in juju – a form of black magic. While true, such stories were also used to make children wary of strangers, in the same way the English talk about the bogeyman.

This Ewe asked me if I knew where I lived and if I could recognize my house when I saw it? I nodded once more terribly frightened. He brought me home by bus. How I do not know, for I had no clue how the bus system worked.

My poor distraught grandmother was pacing up and down, in front of our house, talking loudly to herself, "Yeeaah, Aggie's daughter, how do I explain my case?"

I ran and hugged Nana, and she just held me and swayed and swayed and swayed. She was in a trance. It had been a nightmare for both of us but, she never scolded me. That was the great wonder of my beloved Nana. She understood what I had endured, and her great unending love for me made it so easy for her to understand and forgive, as always.

In our joy at seeing each other, we were so preoccupied with hugging that we completely forgot the policeman, and he discretely left us. I shall be forever grateful to this man for, so to speak, saving my life. This Ewe man proved to me that there is goodness to be found in the most unexpected places. I certainly never made such an impromptu decision again.

The next day at school, the Indian girl and I routinely found ourselves at Assembly, before classes. We both said nothing to each other, but I sensed her discomfort because she knew she had not kept her promise of "the driver will take you home". Secondly, her mother pulling her into the house showed me she was afraid of her, and she felt belittled in front of me. I had witnessed her helplessness. This incident abruptly ended our friendship.

I have never encountered such callousness from an African woman before or since, so I was shocked to find that an Indian woman could behave in such a manner. Later, I came to realise that this was not an isolated incident. Unfortunately, in Ghana and all over Africa, Indians are notorious for their racism, perhaps an extension of their caste system. They seem to think they are several cuts above Africans. On account of this incident, for many years, I distrusted Indians and kept my distance from them. It was only much, much later that this opinion was to change after I met a couple of educated ones.

My parents – who came to Kumasi over the weekends – must have been told of my harrowing experience. The next thing I knew, I was sent off to St Monica's primary boarding school in Mampong, Ashanti Region, for a year. This school was run by European Anglican nuns. The nuns encouraged us to learn cultural dances, and that is how I learnt to dance the cultural dance of the Ashantis, the *adowa*. I am happy to say that I was able to dance the *adowa* at my grandmother's funeral. I felt she would be proud of me for dancing the *adowa* at her funeral.

A year later, my parents moved me back to Kumasi. Maurice and I were enrolled at the Penworth Preparatory School, in Kumasi. It was a co-educational private boarding school, which was unusual at the time. It had separate dormitories for the boys and the girls. This was one of the many mushrooming private schools at the time. It was badly managed, and we were unhappy. We stayed here for only about one term.

I recall my parents reading about Penworth in the newspaper. It offered a lot for low fees. This private primary boarding school even advertised that it would provide an egg a day for breakfast. The fact is, we never saw an egg. The food was never enough for growing children. We were always hungry! I was lucky because some of the teachers favoured me. They would often offer me milk and a cocoa drink after supper. At times, I was given bread or biscuits. I therefore never suffered the great hunger that plagued many of the children, including my brother. The teachers seemed to like my upfront, forthright, and upbeat ways. I saw them as part of the school community, showed interest in them, and spoke easily with them. Many students, however, feared them and tended to shy away.

My parents paid us one of their occasional visits when they came to Kumasi after days in the bush. This time, they asked the headmaster if they could take us home for the weekend. My mother wanted to give my brother a much-needed haircut.

We were delighted. After a good meal at home, Maurice was asked to take off his shirt for the haircut. He removed his shirt.

My mother let out a scream, "My God! What is wrong with you? John, John, come here quickly!"

My brother did not know what he had done wrong. All he had done was to obey our mother's instructions and expose his upper body. His eyes were wide with confusion. I was confused, too, for I was used to seeing him as a pack of bones! Now, I realized something was very wrong. I was asked to take off my clothes too.

"Annette seems OK. How come?" was her dismayed question.

Maurice explained how he was always hungry, and how I was liked by the teachers and was given extra helpings. It was the last time we went to that school. Many other parents followed suit and also pulled out their children. That was the end of Penworth. My brother could not wait to go back to his previous day school – Practice School. This was a local school, in Kumasi, that he loved. It was near our home. Later, he told me that I was not bullied at Penworth, even though I was one of the smallest, because of my relationships with the teachers. I was viewed as a teacher's pet who would tell them everything!

At Penworth, I once remember leaving my dormitory – one tropical rainy day – to pick Maurice up from his dormitory for supper. I found him sitting on the edge of his bed crying and sobbing bitterly. My heart pounded. I felt bad for him. I wanted to protect him.

I blurted out, "Maurice, Maurice, what is wrong? Why are you crying?"

He answered between sobs and the shaking of his little bony shoulders,

"He … , he … , he … , he … ," pointing to the school prefect – the biggest and about the oldest boy in the school – who stood gloating about two metres away, with a smirk on his face, "threw … my … my … jac-ket … in-to … the … rain."

Other students looked on in silence. I looked out of the door and, through the heavy pouring rain, saw his one and only jacket soaked on the dirty, muddy ground outside. I knew what it meant. No supper for him. That was the rule of the school. Supper time meant all boys had to come dressed in clean jackets – just like in the United Kingdom. Girls had to come dressed in clean clothes.

"What did you do?" I managed to stammer, convinced by now of the great wrong done to my gentle brother.

"Nothing," came his sad reply.

Nought could hold me back now. I sprang on the prefect like a wild cat. The goliath of the school was on the floor with everyone looking on. I scratched, kicked, screamed, and pounded him. I had taken him by surprise. In a state of shock and embarrassment, combined with his fear of me being the teachers' darling, he did not retaliate. He got up. I reached for my beloved and shocked brother and led him straight to the teacher-in-charge for the day. Maurice could go in for his supper without a jacket. I, naturally, took the opportunity to inform the teacher about how this prefect abused his position by bullying everyone at school, and he was stripped of his title.

All in all, I must have changed schools at least four times before I ended up at The Technology Primary School in Kumasi. This was one of the best primary schools at the time. After passing the entrance examinations, I started here in the fifth grade. I then proceeded to St Louis Secondary School, Kumasi, at the age of eleven after passing the common entrance exams.

St Louis Secondary School

My Secondary School Years

St Louis Secondary School was run by Catholic nuns from Ireland. Our life there was run like most boarding schools in the country. It was well regimented. However, the environment was easy with the normal pressures during exams. Our daily activities were well planned. We had to attend church daily, before breakfast. The main activity from Monday to Friday was class attendance. At night, we had night studies, doing class work given earlier and preparing for the following day's lessons. Saturdays were free from classes, and we had more time for general and personal chores. The Sunday schedules allowed for time to socialize with our visitors.

Our days started at 06.00 hours with all lights switched on in the dormitories, accompanied by the clapping of hands by the dormitory prefect. We had our times for meals, for chores, for rest, for classes, and for studies. We did have some free time, but it never was for too long. At any time, roll call could be conducted to ensure that all students were present. Although the school was far from town, some students managed to sneak out occasionally. Our days ended at 22.00 hours with lights out in the dormitories.

Our food was prepared in an open air kitchen without windows and doors but with the usual tin roof. Lizards climbed up to the ceiling, and sometimes they would fall into the cooking pots. Whoever got this piece of meat gave a loud yell and jumped up. We would all be disgusted but ate our food all the same. That was all we had.

Secondary school was where I first experienced real hunger. The phrase "going to bed hungry" is indelibly edged in my memory. It was not every day, but it was more often than I care to remember. I was not the only one. My classmates felt the same. Boarding schools do provide three main meals a day. However, growing children do need some snack between meals. Unfortunately, the British and Irish educators were strict about eating between meals.

Food became a preoccupation. Life seemed a constant search for food. Food! Food! Food! This was food to be eaten with bare hands in a common bowl, not because there were no extra bowls and cutlery available, but because traditionally one ate together from a common bowl with one's right hand. Hands were used to pick and spoon food. Gari, shito (local spicy, hot pepper sauce), sardines, corned beef, baked beans, biscuits, and so on and so forth. *Gari soaking* – being a mixture of gari, water, milk, and sugar, sometimes garnished with roasted peanuts – was always eaten with a spoon.

Driven by our unceasing quest for food, we would form alliances with poor hawkers from the neighbouring village. The nuns highly disapproved of their presence in the school, and we all knew this well. These hawkers were our saviours in our daily focus on filling our stomachs. We counted on them as the sole means to supplementing our diet. We needed their food items, and they needed our money. They sold us little buns and *tatre*, a form of fritters made from mashed, ripe plantain. These hawkers also sold us kenkey with fried fish and hot ground pepper.

Undeterred, they would nervously show up behind the dormitories after siesta. Our cat-and-mouse manoeuvres would begin. We would start our business of buying and selling, constantly on the lookout. Business would be interrupted when a student gave a warning sign similar to the hissing of a snake:

"Zzzzzzzzzzzzzz – zzzzzzzzzzz – zzzzzzzzzzzzzzzzzzz!!!"

This meant a nun was approaching. Surrounded by nature, we were capable of imitating some sounds of the animals around.

I remember a girlfriend, Charity, sneaking out of the dormitory one night, past midnight. Charity was usually plagued with hunger. She wanted to buy bread. In full gait and oblivious of the time, she went to the matron's quarters and started to timidly knock at her door:

"Knock! Knock! Knock!" Pause.

"Knock! Knock! Knock!" Pause.

"Knock! Knock! Knock!" Pause.

From within came an impatient, "Who is there?"

"Please matron, do you have bread?" was the timid enquiry.

Charity explained with care who she was and what her mission was.

The sharp, snappy, sarcastic retort from inside was, "It is cheese that I have!!!"

Sunday afternoons from three p.m. to six p.m. was visiting time. This was a welcome change. Not only was it nice receiving visitors, but it also meant receiving food. Food! Food! Extra food! The air was filled with excitement as students moved about with bags of goodies to store away carefully in wooden wardrobes secured with padlocks. There would be plenty of opportunity to eat after the visiting hours.

Whoever had the privilege of getting a visitor was the most popular and valued friend for the day. You suddenly were surrounded by more friends than you remembered. After the visitors left, we all ate fast and wordlessly. Eating was serious business. Within seconds a meal was over. Yet, no one was ever satisfied, only content to have had some snack! For the rest of the evening, the one who had had a visitor was happy and proud to be the centre of attention.

At the end of each term we were all broke. And I mean destitute. Friends scraped together their last pennies to be able to purchase one oily *tatre*. You were very careful to divide it into equal portions. To do otherwise could cost you a friend. These were rules outside of the classroom that you did not break.

Some photographers came to pick up some business at the school. We loved having our pictures taken. There were no such things as school pictures. In retrospect, these pictures are documents of interesting phases in our lives. They captured a time in our development.

Girlfriends

St Louis Secondary School, in Kumasi, was where I spent the longest time in my school career. I started there in form one and completed the sixth form. I have very fond memories from this period of my life. Gifted with a good amount of emotional intelligence, I had a feel for people, and being someone who liked socializing more than reading, I made friends easily. I was fond of my schoolmates, and I believe I was pretty well liked in return. I found people of all cultures and backgrounds interesting. They intrigued me. Like most students, we did not have much in the way of material possessions. We met at a time in our lives where personalities mattered. I saw a lot of good in people. My schoolmates were individuals with different characters and personalities. Some were bossy, and some were quick tempered. Some had too much confidence, and some had none. Some were very sensitive, and others were insensitive. Some were paranoid, and some did not give a damn. We did not only give our teachers nicknames, but we also nicknamed each other. My nickname of "Oburoni Dongee" meant I did not give a damn. We were all, however, an interesting and fun group.

Being of a free nature gave me a certain amount of openness to people. I was not only friendly, but also did not hesitate to stand up to anyone – be it a classmate, senior, or a teacher – when I felt wronged. I was never physical but would clearly and objectively defend myself, without fear. In Ghanaian society, however, children were taught not to confront older people.

In retrospect, the choice of my two best friends, reflect who I am: a child of both cultures. One of these girlfriends was Beatrice Appiah-Kusi, an Ashanti. No one could explain to me better the Ashanti customs. She answered my many questions, simply and clearly, with patience. The other best friend, Beatrice Aboley, was from the northern part of Ghana. She lost both parents at a very early age and was raised by two American missionary doctors, giving her a more westernised background. These two girlfriends made a great impact on me. Like me, they were free spirits.

Lessons from Boarding School

I practically grew up in boarding schools, so my life was greatly influenced by this educational system. I learnt a lot from life in boarding schools. You were responsible for yourself in many ways. Our meals were prepared for us. However, we did everything else ourselves. We kept the footpaths swept clean. In addition, we kept our dormitories and classrooms clean. We did our own washing and ironing. Some of us were better than others in doing these chores. Rose, a classmate, was good at ironing clothes, and this gave her enormous pride. By the time she finished ironing her starched uniforms, they could practically stand up all by themselves!

Rules are important guidelines for a child. Too many rules are, however, counterproductive. It does not help a child to be truly independent, but our secondary school seemed to be too regimented. There were rules for this and rules for that. Sometimes, it even seemed teachers made up rules right there on the spot! Should you be caught breaking these rules, you suffered the consequences. One of these was being made to stand in the baking tropical sun for hours without a drop of water. For European sun worshipers, it might not appear to be a punishment, but to us, born and bred in the tropics, it was a severe punishment.

Despite the abundant rules, we enjoyed a tranquil school environment. There was no feeling of oppression, and you could be yourself. You could flourish and be successful in any pursuit and endeavour of your choice – academics, sports, theatre or cultural dance, debating society, the choir, and so on.

Like most students, I had few possessions and even less money. So, I learnt to be frugal. I also learnt very early to take care of what few possessions I had. I felt secure in myself and really enjoyed socializing with my friends and participating in the various activities I delighted in, like sports, acting, and debating. However, I also knew when it was time to hit the books.

There was little communication with the outside world, so we were protected and lived in isolation from the *real* world. Leaving secondary school for the world was like an awakening. I believe this may have been a challenge for some of us transitioning into the *real* life. Suddenly, the rules that governed your daily life were no longer apparent. You were free. You were on your own.

I did think about life after secondary school. We all had our aspirations and dreams about what we wanted out of life. I remember thinking academics was fine, but it was not the sole road to success in life. Success in life for me was in business. I was influenced by relatives and family friends who were in business. With this ambition in mind, I looked at going abroad as a goal. This was where I could start to realize my ambitions.

I decided I wanted to be a secretary. My brother Maurice, who had left earlier to attend the Swiss Federal Institute of Technology in Zurich on a full scholarship, was able to work during the holidays and earn good money. He offered to pay my fees at the secretarial school. The first step was to look for a good secretarial school in Britain. It was too late for me to enter this secretarial school shortly after secondary school because we applied too late. So I had to wait a year. During this time, I worked at the Standard Bank of Ghana in Accra to help pay for my flight to London.

My parents had moved to Accra a few years earlier, when I was about fifteen years old. My stepfather got a job outside the timber business, so Accra became our new city. My memory of this town is limited to the holidays and the couple of months I worked there. So, I never really got to know it well.

Chapter Three: Trip to London

My first trip abroad was to London in 1972. I had heard many stories, good and bad, from family members and schoolmates who had had the privilege of going abroad for some of their holidays. The bright city lights of London spelled freedom for me. Prior to this time, I had led a protected and secluded life. We were controlled twenty-four hours a day in boarding school, through roll calls and sporadic checks by the nuns. At home, there were no nuns, but it was no better. Our parents were strict, because they wanted to avert teenage pregnancy. Home was always where we had to be. Should we venture out for some reason, we had to account for our whereabouts. Gosh, was it boring! We could scream from boredom. There was nothing to do all day: read, converse, eat, read, talk, eat, and sleep.

As my older brother, Charles, once commented, "As for you girls, you are really camped!"

This is Ghanaian English for "you are always kept in the house".

That was an understatement. We really did not mind the overprotection, but it was boring. There was Ghana TV and European music. There were also English books and comics to read. Our parents occasionally took us girls to parties thrown by their friends. As their friends were not our peers, we did not really enjoy ourselves.

The bright city lights of London meant a fun night life to me. I got to love night clubs. I loved to dance. I remember once literally dancing all night in a London club. In the end, my feet could not hold me up. The fashionable high clogs that I wore did not help either. I had to be carried home by friends.

London also held some fears for me. I recalled the tales of Jack the Ripper. This was the city where he committed those gruesome crimes against women. I had to be careful here.

I arrived at Heathrow airport one dark, wet October evening. Passengers finally poured out of the Ghana Airways plane. In silence, we moved in tandem towards the baggage claim section. I claimed my luggage and dragged it through the exit doors. The cold autumn wind whipped through my thin summer trousers and my five feet, five inch and one hundred pound frame. I was chilled to the bone, and I knew for sure that I was no longer in the tropics.

Everything looked grey and black. The people dressed, accordingly, in grey and black. My mother's friend, Auntie Elizabeth, was out there to meet me.

(This was not her real name. The names in this section have been changed to protect identities.)

She had arranged for a friend of hers to help pick me up in his car. She was also dressed in grey and black. As we drove to her flat, I observed the streets and houses. Everything looked so old and grey. The city seemed so dead.

Auntie Elizabeth must have read the look of disappointment on my face for she said, "Annette, this is what the western world is all about. You will get used to it".

I had no response.

We finally arrived at her flat which was in a grey building in

Balham. She opened the door to that little room they called home. The flat consisted of one room. There were several rented rooms in this building. There was, however, only one bathroom and one toilet for all the tenants.

My mouth must have dropped because Auntie Elizabeth added, "*Ewuraba* [lady], here no one lives in houses like back home."

I was speechless. If I could have beamed myself back home, that would have been the end of my life in this part of the world.

Auntie Elizabeth was about twenty years older than my mother. She was tall and heavy. In build, she was big and had the typical broad hips and big back side of many Ghanaian women. Her figure was like the usual guitar-shaped elderly woman, with a slight waddle when she moved. Auntie Lizzy, as she was at times called, was lively and could joke. Her bulging expressive eyes, oblong face, and full African lips that dropped as need be during narrations, made her even more amusing to observe. All throughout her years in London, Auntie Elizabeth stayed true to her Ghanaian habit of wearing the traditional *kaba* and cloth, with a head kerchief. When it got colder, she would wear a pullover. At such times, she wore a heavy coat to go out.

Auntie Elizabeth was a Fante, from the coastal area of Ghana. Like many Fantes, she had moved around a bit in Ghana. She had spent many of her earlier years in Kumasi. It was here, according to her narration, that she and her Ghanaian husband were to part forever. She recounts how she had met her husband's young lover, at Kingsway department store in Kumasi. Auntie Lizzy, who was almost six feet tall and well built, was a mother of three. She said not only did she beat the living daylights out of this woman, but she also stripped her naked by tearing off the clothes on her rival's back. When her husband heard of it, he claimed she had disgraced him in public by not behaving like a lady and that was the end of their marriage.

My mother befriended Auntie Elizabeth years later when Auntie was married to a broke old English man in Accra. Her husband, Smith, was known as "bore hole" by my stepfather and his English friends, because they found him to be extremely boring. Smith claimed he owned two houses in London. How Auntie Lizzy could believe this was a puzzle to us all. Even in Ghana, where life was pretty easy financially for most Europeans, Smith still continued to live in cheap hostels. After marriage, Auntie Lizzy continued living in her poor quarters. Fact is Auntie Lizzy's biggest ambition was to get to the UK where her two oldest sons had settled. Besides going abroad was the dream and goal of many. Little did she know what life was going to be like in the U.K.

In London, Smith is said to have vanished, and Auntie Elizabeth, with a British passport that could be obtained those days, immediately after marriage to a Briton, found herself on the dole. She was first given a room in Balham, a poor part of London, for herself and Agatha, her daughter and last born. This was when I first went to London. Here I was to spend a couple of months until a room became available at my school's hostel. Here I shared the only bed with Agatha and Auntie Lizzy slept on her old settee. There were no wardrobes available, so my clothes remained in my suitcase.

Life was pretty tough. Finally, it was at the school's hostel's rented room that I was to first have a wardrobe and a bed, all to myself. The shared bathroom there was pleasantly clean.

Years later, the council gave Auntie Elizabeth and her daughter a small house in the same area that had become available. Little did she know what a nightmare this would also turn out to be. Heavy rains turned her bedroom, on the ground floor, into a pool with everything in the room afloat. Eventually, she was given a better place.

After a long absence, during which she did not know where her husband was, he one day appeared at her doorstep. She was surprised to see him, and in all her anger and frustration, she threw a bucket of water at him and that was the last time she heard of him.

Auntie Elizabeth was constantly mixing her Fante and English in her speech, and I had the impression she did not even realise it. The adaptation of British ways and speech had been so integrated in her Fante life that it had become part of her whole being. Like many immigrants, before she came abroad, her constant talk and ambition was to live in London and to escape the poverty in Ghana. However, after seeing how awful life was on the dole, she changed her tune, and she talked constantly of going back to Ghana to settle and buy a small house for her old age. Fate had it that she eventually could go back to Ghana on a visit and buy a piece of land, but, unfortunately, she died shortly after her return to the UK in the 1980s.

My impression of London, prior to my visit, was the London I saw in the movies – a glamorous London. What I now saw and experienced was the opposite. I was so disappointed. I was so miserable. Everything seemed so ancient and run down. At home, in Ghana, I was used to seeing smiling people dressed in bright colours. Here, the faces did not smile at you. There was no show of emotion. These solemn people reflected the grey and miserable environment. It was depressing. No, I wanted my Ghana back. I missed the sunshine. I missed the smiling people. I made up my mind that, as soon as I had completed my college, I would head back to Ghana.

For the first time, I saw white people cleaning streets and doing menial jobs. At first it seemed strange. In Ghana, I was used to black people doing such jobs with the white people in managerial positions. Is this real? Can I believe what I am seeing? Of course, how stupid! What am I thinking? It made sense. This is their country and they should manage their land. Why should the black always do the dirty jobs?

It was autumn, and I was in desperate need of warm clothing. I had to buy winter clothes as soon as possible. My summer clothes were just not warm enough. I discovered the shopping centre. Knightsbridge, Park Lane, Baker Street, and – and – and – all with luxury shops. There was one beautiful shop after another – in rows and on opposite sides of neat, well-kept streets. The clothes were as beautiful as those I had seen in English glamour magazines. I fell in love with shopping in London. I felt I had arrived. Now, I was in the middle of it all and could spend hours going from shop to shop at every opportunity. But, I could only afford a few items and a black coat – like most people. This was in a middle-class shop on Oxford Street. It was explained to me by the friendly sales girls and women that a black or dark coat hid the dirt better and one could wear it all through winter. It could be dry-cleaned when the season was over.

So, this was the reason why most people wore these earthy colours! Practicality has its place. I could only afford one coat, so I had to join them. My desire for a brightly coloured coat to cheer me up had to wait. It was strange, at first, to be addressed as "Dear" and "Love" by the sales girls. Later on, I got used to it and even found it sweet.

I needed warm shoes for the winter if I were to have warm feet. I set out looking at the various shoe shops. There were shoes for everyone, from grandmothers to the most fashionable. They had practical, comfortable shoes. They also had shoes whose sole purpose must have been to make some kind of a fashion statement – like "Look at what I can stand up on!" Some of those platform shoes had heels measuring up to ten inches and more.I was used to wearing practical shoes in Ghana. I therefore made a practical choice at a shop in Balham. The friendly sales girl advised me once again that my choice was absolutely not in, and I would be the laughing stock of my peers. Now, that I did not want, so I decided, "If you cannot beat them, join them." I made a compromise. I bought a pair of clogs. About five-inch heel was as high as I could walk in without feeling too ridiculous.

My College, The Queen's Secretarial College, at Queensberry Place, was located in an upscale section of London. School started. In order to get there, from Balham, I needed to take public transportation. It was my first day, and I set out in my black coat and clogs carrying my heavy books. It was rush hour. Traffic was heavy. The red, double-decker bus – on which I found myself – was packed. There was barely room to even stand. Not being very big, I felt squashed from all sides. It was claustrophobic. The bus seemed to bully its way through the traffic and then close to my school, it stopped for what seemed a while.

I figured that must be a bus stop, so I squeezed my way through the standing crowd, in the lower part of the bus, and jumped out just as the bus started to move forward with a jolt, causing all people sitting and standing to sway forwards and backwards. I fell right on my butt with my books and other items scattered around me on the street. I was shocked, annoyed and angry with the stupid driver. Thoroughly shaken, I picked up my belongings between rushing cars. I had not jumped out at a bus stop but in traffic. The bus stop was about fifty feet away!

Well, I learned my lesson, and from then on, I knew what a bus stop should look like in London. Traffic rules were very strict, and buses only stopped for passengers to get out at these stops and no where else – not an inch before!

It was in these red, double-decker buses of London that I first saw people talking to themselves. Having led a sheltered life in Ghana, I was fascinated to see this. They held complete conversations all by themselves, with questions and answers, using different tones of voices. They were oblivious to the world around them, and people ignored them.

It was while riding the public transportation systems (the underground and buses) that I also first noticed people who kept blinking and twitching their faces. I interpreted it as nerve problems. I summed it up as a direct result of the many stresses of this society that must have affected them in some way. People tend to be private and do not divulge their problems or irritations. They will not readily let you know the stresses they endure. Were they able to be open in discussing or communicating their problems, they probably would find relief. They would find it to be beneficial.

In Ghana, you could meet a total stranger at a bus stop who would actually start talking to you, engaging you in a discussion, seeking your opinion, about his or her personal problems: "Lady (or gentleman), please just listen to my case …."

Although that advice may not be taken, that person is letting off steam – venting his or her feelings. They part, probably, never to see each other again and forgetting the whole encounter. However, the listener may also have benefited from this interaction. Perhaps, in a way to better solve one's own problems or in gaining some insight in life's ways. The point in letting off steam is helpful and everyone understands it is necessary in Ghana. And all this was achieved without once setting foot in the office of some therapist – without waiting for an appointment and without paying! In Ghana, I never heard of a therapist. People usually tend to be patient and tend to take time to listen to each other.

My college was very small and exclusive. I was the only black student. Most people here spoke the Queen's English and many of the students came from the British upper class. They were called "Lady" this and "Lady" that there. Some of these students were featured in magazines as debutantes. You could see their lavish homes and castles as backdrops in the pictures. Christina Onassis – the daughter of the richest man in the world, at the time, was said to have been a student here. Fergie, the Duchess of York, is said to have also studied here. The students were civil and nice, and there was small talk in school, between breaks, but I was never invited to their world. I made friends with two girls but lost touch after college.

Before coming to London, I was under the impression Ghana was Africa. Other countries on the African continent existed but were uninteresting. I was therefore taken aback when someone asked me whether I knew a person living in Johannesburg, South Africa, after hearing I was from Africa. This question showed me how little some Europeans knew about Africa. South Africa and Ghana are thousands of miles apart. It also made me aware that South Africa was a very important land for the western hemisphere, and that Ghana was known to very few people here and was not as important for the rest of Europe as I had thought. These revelations disappointed me but did not reduce my love for my Ghana.

In Ghana, it was considered OK for men to smoke. A woman who smoked was usually considered a tart. Cigarettes are retailed singly in Ghana. One can buy a whole packet, of course, but most people cannot afford this. So they would buy one or two cigarettes. At times these men would even share a cigarette.

Shortly after moving in to the college hostel, I was invited by one of the students to a party in the building. Upon entering, I noticed there was no music playing and there was no dancing. People just stood around talking to each other. There was, however, a lot of drinking just like in Ghana. Unlike Ghana, the English girls were not reserved, but talked, flirted, and even kissed openly with the young men. Their cheerfulness showed their good party mood. It also dawned on me how most of the girls were smoking with the guys. I sensed they wanted to be cool. They kept passing cigarettes to one another after taking a long puff. I took it to be because they were *broke* like myself, and could not afford the luxury of buying a pack of cigarettes. I was not used to drinking and not wanting to make a fool of myself, hardly drank much. I was friendly and polite, but reserved. In the course of the evening, I was asked whether I wanted a smoke. I replied, "No thanks, I do not smoke". Later, I was to learn it meant smoke a joint. I guess that is why someone once said to me, "You're very bourgeois". Me? Bourgeois? Truth is they were rebelling against *their* society. And, I was trying to survive in *their* society. But, how were they to know? How were they to understand? I was never invited to such a party again, and that was OK with me. I guess I have always felt confident in what is good for me. I have never believed in keeping up with the Joneses.

One of the customs of social London etiquette stunned me: when you were invited to come over, it was not a dinner invitation. If you happened to still be around at supper time, the hosts would excuse themselves to go and have dinner, while offering you a drink. At first, I was shocked and found it odd, but it was an eye opener. As they say in Ghana, travel and see. Back home, in Ghana, when invited to come over, it was a dinner invitation. It was also normal for visitors to walk in any time of the day. They were always made to feel welcome. If you happened to drop in on a family eating, a place would be quickly made for you. You would be made to feel like they had been waiting for you all along.

I found out later that in Switzerland or Germany, when one was invited for a drink, then it was for a drink; for a meal, then a meal was included. On the other hand, people in Asia are extremely hospitable. They never stop feeding their guests for fear they will leave thinking they were not good enough hosts. I remember visiting India and Singapore on business. We seemed to do nothing but eat. I was bursting, and still food was being pushed on us. I just could not see or smell food anymore.

Since I was broke, it became obvious shortly after arriving in London that I needed a part-time job to help see me through college. Soon, I found one, working on Saturdays. It was at a shop known as Selfridges, at one of the many perfume stands. I was excited about the possibility of earning some extra money. To my surprise and delight I was told I did not have to pay taxes as what I earned weekly was way below the minimum taxable limit. Making it to this shop very early in the cold months was not easy. I was not used to the cold and really felt it. I however enjoyed each care-free day there. I had my own stand and was my own boss.

Never having owned perfume before in my life and fascinated by the scents, I started and ended each day by trying all the perfumes available from the sample bottles! I was a walking perfumery, and I just loved it. Working and making my own money taught me a good lesson about a lifetime goal – financial independence. Having your own money means not being beholden to anyone. You can control and manage your life. This gives one a certain amount of pride and confidence.

A visit to the pub was a must, and I routinely went to pubs with friends, over the weekends, to unwind after five days of relentless studying. It seemed normal to pop in for a pint – draft of pint or half of bitter, lager or a dark Guinness. Not used to alcohol, I never exceeded one pint. Many English pubs were usually furnished with old furniture that had seen many generations come and go. The pubs were usually overcrowded, and they did not have enough seating available, so you stood around the bar. The pubs in general were not very clean, but after a pint you did not notice. You left the pub at the magic hour of eleven p.m. It was when I went to Switzerland that I realised that the toilets in English pubs were filthy by comparison. It was brought home to me forcibly again, when years later I visited London for my mother's funeral. I held out as long as possible before going to the loo.

One of my first encounters with the government laws and regulations in England involved the pub hours. Promptly at eleven p.m., the pub owner had to throw every customer out, otherwise he stood the chance of losing his license. This was understood by all. I was to encounter more laws that governed the everyday lives of people in this part of the world. At first, I was perplexed but impressed by how law abiding they were. It was not like Ghana where some people seemed to think that the laws were non-binding suggestions. In Ghana there are laws governing the operating hours of bars, but no one observes them and the government does not enforce them.

I had heard that London had a fish and chips shop at every corner. I could not wait to try them. I did, and to my surprise found them pretty tasteless and oily. I preferred the Chinese take-a-ways that were competing with the fish and chips stands. The Chinese meals were spicier and easier for me to digest. All in all, Chinese fast food was a life saver. Not only did it suit the budget, but after a hard day's work, going shopping and cooking in the evenings was an extra strain one preferred to avoid.

Tropical rains are heavy and of a short duration. People stay indoors until the rains stop. They usually manage without umbrellas and raincoats. Here in London, an umbrella or raincoat was a necessity for it never stopped raining. It was usually a light downpour or a drizzle, and trying to sit out the rains inside would be pointless. Everyone owned an umbrella or a raincoat. Most people had both. At such moments, I could have all I wanted that this city could offer, but I could never have a good hair-do. Having fly-away hair, it was often messy.

London was very class conscious and clearly had racial issues. The area where you lived seemed to determine your status in society. I remember going flat hunting, after completing college, with my best girlfriend, Susan. We looked for a flat in the good areas of London. She, being English and with a good English accent, would always call to find out first whether a flat was still available for two people. As soon as they saw me the flat was gone. We soon realised the problem and decided to check it out. She would call the same place where the flat was taken to find it was still available. In the end, after trying over and over again and failing, we decided to look for a flat separately. Sure enough, she got one immediately.

I never had a chance to flat share with English girls. The only chance I eventually had to live in a middle-class area was through flat sharing with foreigners. Otherwise, I would have ended up in one of the many ghettos of London. This was a big lesson to me, and I was ever determined to either make it well in the western world or go back home to Ghana. A black person with no money in this part of the world experienced discrimination daily. When blacks walked into a hotel, even the waiters looked at them as if to say, "What do you want?" or "You do not belong here!"

It was in London that I became aware of the noise levels in my surroundings. I learned it was normal not to be loud. Being loud in public was strongly discouraged. It was viewed as disturbing the peace, and this was against the law. I learned you were not to laugh too loudly or talk too loudly. People whispered to each other in public places – like in church, at the theatre, or at museums. A visit to a restaurant meant talking loud enough to be heard only at your given table and not beyond. This also applied to laughing. Loud laughter in these places was frowned upon. People had a right to quiet surroundings.

What a sharp contrast to my gregarious, boisterous, Ghana. Attending cinemas in Ghana, I recalled how the audience would identify and loudly empathize with the characters on the screen. If the scene was sad they wept. If it was funny they laughed. If the character accomplished some great feat there was audible relief. In London, the audience probably experienced the same emotions, but they were quieter.

Unlike Ghana, people in London were not used to a lot of noise. Whoever disturbed the peace could be reported by neighbours to the police, whose duty it was to also ensure there was peace among the citizens. It was, therefore, a good idea to invite the neighbours if you anticipated having a noisy party. Angry neighbours just notified the police. Peace and quiet were especially important in the residential areas of London. In your home you were expected to conduct your activities mindful of the noise that might disturb your neighbour. Children were not exempt. Loudness was not accepted from them either. A neighbour could call the police and lodge a complaint against you if you were too loud in your home. This included family quarrels heard from your home. Unheard of in Ghana! There, the first step would be for someone to intervene and try to help, or to eavesdrop with the intention of gossiping later.

While riding the public transportation systems, I further observed the quiet ways in which people conducted themselves. The English are very private. People either kept quiet or read newspapers, books, or magazines. If they spoke it was in low tones. Even the traffic noise appeared to be controlled despite the numerous vehicles. They did not honk their horns, and they had good mufflers for their exhaust pipes, unlike Ghana. I remember once standing at a street corner. I heard an African boy exclaim to his mother, "Don't the cars, taxis and buses here have horns?"

I imagined how traffic would come to a complete halt in Ghana if vehicles had no horns to blast. They are necessary because of the limited pedestrian crossings and the people's penchant for crossing the roads without looking. I believe in Ghana they are a safety issue.

Having grown up with an Englishman who spoke the Queen's English and having been in the company of his many British friends, I thought I knew the Queen's English very well. Imagine my shock and embarrassment when I sometimes found it hard to understand my English classmates and friends and acquaintances. I started wondering whether we spoke inferior English in Ghana. Not so, when I realised that the English also found it difficult to understand foreigners whose English was different from theirs. With time, I was able to understand them better.

In the course of my stay in London, I met people from other English speaking countries who also initially found the English difficult to understand. It took me a while to fully understand Americans, Australians, and other English speakers. I was completely confused when an American woman asked me where the "restroom" was at the railway station. I thought she meant the waiting room and directed her to the waiting room behind us. She was irritated and finally said toilet. It was also interesting for me to note that the English used "loo" for toilet.

To me, the English were forever saying "thank you" and "I'm sorry" not because they were really thankful or sorry but they were just being polite and mannerly.

I find the English are generally brought up to be civil and polite. Unlike Germans, they are not blunt and direct. They usually do not call a spade a spade. They beat about the bush and tend not to open up too much. They are reserved in many ways, and it is sometimes difficult for foreigners dealing with them to know where they stand.

Step by step, I learned to find my way about. I mastered the bus and underground system. Minding my business did not bother me either. I did not need to be gregarious. We all just moved about like zombies in a rat race. With time, I liked this silence, for I was better focused. No one broke my train of thought, and no one disturbed me. In time, I picked up my pace and was just as fast as everyone around me. Not necessarily because I had to keep time. This was necessary if you wanted to keep warm. Rushing gets you to a warmer and dryer spot more quickly. Ghana is warm all year round, and people take their time in moving from one spot to another.

I was focused and determined in pursuing my goals. I took advantage of opportunities that came my way. Living in London was lonely, and I felt I was a long way from home. But, I had a purpose. What aided me was my inner strength and sense of balance. They guided me in pursuing what was right for Annette. I never felt I had to compete with anyone. Jealousy and envy never consumed me. I was always busy trying to be myself and figuring out what I wanted out of life.

People are creatures of habit. As time went by, I got used to the grey and wet days with the matching grey rows of houses. In the autumn and winter, I rarely saw the sun. I went to college in darkness and left it in darkness in the late afternoons. You just managed. Life was busy, fast, and expensive. My focus was to stay in the race and stay happy.

I slowly discovered what made London so famous and fascinating. Yes, the buildings might be old and grey, but they are solid. Within them is usually a different world. Some are very modern, though many are moderate inside and at times still have archaic plumbing systems. The shops are world renowned with something for everyone's pocket. There are luxury shops that sell designer products from Armani, Dior, Louis Vuitton, Burberry, Ralph Lauren, Gucci, and Versace. There are also cheaper shops in Shepherd's Bush and other places that are stocked with imports from Asia. The sky is the limit for what you can buy here. There are parks, famous museums like Madame Tussauds with their wax figures of the famous, from the past to the present. There are art galleries and museums reflecting the wealth and acquisitions of the British Empire of long ago.

There is something for every one. It is up to you to find what you want. The reality is that very few people can really afford to live well here and for the vast majority it is a life of living from hand to mouth. Some parts of London are said to have the most expensive pieces of ground in the world! It is a cosmopolitan city and has something for all the various ethnic groups. Yes, this city also has its charm and interesting places that one learns to like and appreciate. No one ever feels out of place. We all seem to feel like we belong.

After college, I looked for a job. In the meantime, I worked as a temporary secretary in various firms, through an employment agency. Eventually, I got employed as secretary at the Sierra Leone Embassy in London. My brother Maurice had paid for my secretarial studies, and I felt obliged to pay for my sister Brenda's fees, too, and get her settled in London before school started for her. After studying the economic and social situation in the UK, I did not want to spend the rest of my life here. So, late in 1974, I left London by train to visit my brother, Maurice, in Zurich. My intention was to return to Ghana via Switzerland.

Chapter Four: Visiting Switzerland

Switzerland is a small country in Central Europe. It is landlocked. To the north is Germany; Austria lies to the east; Italy is to the south and France to the west. It is made up predominantly of mountains: the Jura in the west and the Alps, which cover most of eastern Switzerland. The low lands between the Jura and the Alps is where most Swiss people live. I call Switzerland the land of tunnels because the network of very good roads is connected through the many tunnels in the mountains.

Switzerland is made up of twenty-six states known as cantons. There are four official languages – German, French, Italian, and Rhaeto-Romanic. Rhaeto-Romanic is said to have its roots in the Latin. Some say, it is a mixture of German, French and Italian. Switzerland is politically very stable. For this reason many international organisations have their headquarters here.

I had to see Switzerland, the land of my forefathers. London was so close, and this was a lifetime chance that might never come again, I thought. I arrived one cold, miserable November night by train with all my worldly possessions in a suitcase of not more than twenty kilograms in weight.

So this is the famous Zurich, I said to myself. Zurich is one of the best-known European cities. The people spoke Swiss-German. It sounded so guttural, rough, and strong. Faces on the streets were less cosmopolitan. There were not so many blacks in this city. It was clean, but unlike London, the buildings were more modern. I was used to the London buses and tubes and so was initially confused by the trams in Zurich. Trams ran on electrical cables, the sight of which unnerved me because I was afraid they would fall and electrocute me. All those tram lines on the ground were also confusing because I did not know when it was safe to cross. Finding myself on the side of the street, with my brother, I moved my head in all directions. I tried to cross and in my confusion I almost got run over by a tram and had to jump back for dear life. With time, I got used to it.

Unexpected Changes

After three months in Zurich I was just about penniless. I had entered this country for a visit with a return ticket to Ghana and a couple of English pounds sterling, in my pocket, knowing I was going to live off Maurice and his Swiss girlfriend - in some corner, in their flat – expecting free meals. I got the free meals and free accommodation from them. It could not, however, last forever.

I decided to stay for a while in Switzerland and learn French. If so, I needed a job badly. I had no money and no one to finance my studies. This was at a time when bilingual secretaries, trained abroad, were in demand not only in Ghana but also in the Ivory Coast, a neighbouring former French colony. The salaries for these secretaries were sometimes much better than those of many graduates from the universities. I was still young, and there was no reason for me to rush home. Geneva was my next goal. Give me a helping hand, and I will help myself! I found a job through my brother's contacts in Geneva. This was as secretary at the Nigerian Mission to the United Nations in Geneva in early 1975.

This employment gave me a diplomatic permit to stay and work in Geneva. This was good because a Ghanaian passport, without a visa or a permit, would have meant a one-way-ticket home, to Accra, Ghana. I saw this as a chance in a lifetime. I immediately enrolled at the "Migros" evening school to learn French.

Geneva was cosmopolitan. The United Nations offices here

had people of all races, colours, and creeds. It was cleaner than London and everything was in French. The signs and advertisements, as well as the television programmes, were all in French. French was also very present at the United Nations, but one could get by with English, that being the first language at the UN. Geneva had trams too, but I was used to them by now. Traffic was quicker and faster here, for the drivers drove in an erratic fashion like the French in France. One had to pay more attention to the cars than to the trams here. Here I felt at home. My friends were mixed. They were of all races. Discrimination was not so bad here. But it was present. This time it was not so much the colour of your skin, but more your economic status. Life was very expensive, but my St Louis days of no money and always being broke had taught me how to budget and make it last. Life was good. Unlike London, I could afford my own little flat. Every working person could afford their own little place. Like England, it was unusual for a foreigner to share a flat with a Swiss, unless it was with a boy or girlfriend.

I began my French lessons in the evenings. It was a necessity. Five years of French in school and no one here could understand my French. My Ghanaian / English accent in French was so bad that it was beyond comprehension. All I ever got back from my piece of French communication was, "Pardon Madame. Je ne comprends pas" – meaning, "Excuse me, madam. I do not understand".

Unlike Ghana, where the system of language learning is initially more concentrated on the written forms, I learnt here that the first approach is to understand what is said and to pronounce words correctly. The right pronunciation is important to get the right accent in any language. This, I find, is the key to speaking any language well.

Learning French was a twice a week drill that I dreaded. Each lesson was for two hours in the evenings – after work. We were first taught comprehension and pronunciation from our books. No one ever missed their chance of being singled out in class to display their knowledge and understanding. Then the worst part of the evening began. It was like being put in a drill chamber. You were alone in a cabin with ear phones on and a computer teacher that had no mercy. It never understood a wrong pronunciation or accepted the slightest error in a sentence. Mistakes meant repetition and repetition meant no progress. Your fight was with this damn computer the rest of the evening. It was a relief when this bout was over each time. Surprisingly enough, it was my best teacher, and each drill session gave me a sense of progress and satisfaction.

I moved on at the age of twenty-three to be the secretary of the Ghanaian ambassador to the United Nations and Switzerland in June 1975. I was said to be the youngest secretary to an ambassador in Geneva, during the Kissinger era. This was a time in history when the world community started again to see the importance of the African continent. Mr Kissinger, of the United States of America, was the most powerful minister of foreign affairs. It was a period in history of the Cold War between the western democratic world and the eastern communist world. The two world powers, America and the Soviet Union, were fighting for more influence in the various countries of this planet.

My secretarial position offered me more contacts with people of other nationalities from all over the world. I realized once more that countries where the English language was the official form of communication all had their special ways of pronunciation and special expressions. Nigerians spoke English with a heavier and more rounded accent than Ghanaians. Americans sounded different from Canadians. Australians spoke like Cockneys – only more clearly – and I sometimes found it difficult to understand them. All people from the Caribbean countries sounded different from each other. Among themselves they spoke patois, English mixed with other languages. This is pidgin English that is very unique and different from the pidgin English spoken in West Africa. Both black and white South Africans spoke differently, as well.

After a childhood of wanting to meet different races, I found most of them here in Geneva. We did not only work together, we also found ourselves at cocktail receptions during the week and partied at the weekends. I like people, and it was easy for me to get along with these people from different nations. I discovered we were really all alike. At the end of the day, our aspirations were the same. We got sad, we laughed, we wanted recognition, and we pursued our goals. We were all part of mankind.

My First Fight

Geneva was also where I first had a fight as an adult. It was on an evening boat trip across Lake Geneva. I was with a couple of Ghanaian friends. My brother and his Swiss then-girlfriend were visiting from Zurich. We were all in a good mood. The sailing boat was brightly lit up, and the band was playing this Saturday evening. Having the rhythm in our blood, we could not sit still and left our two tables for the dance floor. My brother was the first to leave the dance floor to sit down.

A Swiss couple had taken a seat at one of our tables. This was not a problem. Maurice, my brother, motioned to the woman that he wanted to move past her to the now available space, by the window. Her suspicious partner misunderstood this polite gesture and took it as a pass at his woman. He whacked Maurice on the head. Maurice stepped back, with eyes opened wide, in surprise. I may have been grooving, but I had caught the scene. I stepped forward to the woman and gestured with my hands – in my Ghanaian way – demanding, "Qu'est-ce que c'est?" Meaning, "what is the problem?" She slapped me. She did not know what she had started. I jumped back on my high heels, legs spread apart in a defensive posture. Before anyone of our friends could react I had, in a flash, whacked the woman's head. She screamed and held her head. Her partner was now out of his depth. He was panicking and yelling, "Elle a frappe ma femme!" – "She has hit my wife!"

The band stopped playing. The dance floor cleared. Now, complete silence prevailed. The security people on the boat rushed to the scene. Everyone was told to leave the boat. We, the fighters, were asked to remain on board. This made me realize that the round trip was over and that we had returned to Geneva and were docking. The passengers moved away from us like we had the plaque. Their quick, stolen glances emphasized their disgust. We watched everyone disembark and saw the police speed boat racing towards us with the lights flashing.

They beckoned us to go with them to the water-police station, a couple of miles away. This was a matter for them and not a case for the police on land! This was new to me. Another form of division of labour! We found ourselves on the speedboat, zooming across this lake where everything around us was pitch black except for the flashing lights of the police boat and the far away lights across the lake, representing the houses and town around this lake. I was quiet. Our Swiss opponent's raving and ranting gave him away, and the police men advised him to forget the case for it was clear he had a problem with foreigners and that I had reacted in self-defence. It was obvious that they had initiated the brawl.

Meeting my Swiss Aunt

I have said a lot about my black roots in previous chapters. This is because Ghana is where I was born and bred. Truth be told, I did not know much about my father and Switzerland.

The real question of interest that had preoccupied me for a lifetime was who was my father? Who was this father that had died so young? A man that was never around to love and see his children grow up. A papa I loved and missed throughout my childhood. I never stopped yearning for him. I fantasized he was watching me with the pride and joy of a loving father in a make believe world, my little childhood secret. Yes, children need both parents. Never make that mistake. I needed and missed this as a child. I missed the unconditional love of a father, growing up – love that saw no wrong in you. The most perfect form of love – loving and giving with no expectations. What was he really like? How was his life before he came to Ghana? I was never to know firsthand.

Well, I finally met my Swiss aunt – Alice Julia Bürgin – in Locarno, in the summer of 1976. Locarno is located on the northern tip of Lake Maggiore, at the foot of the Alps, in the Swiss canton (state) of Tessin. Italian is the official language here. Maurice and his Swiss then-girlfriend, my German boyfriend – later my husband – and I visited her and her husband. They were retired. Tante Alice, as we called her, was my father's elder sister and only sibling. Bürgin was her married name. She was about my height, heavy in structure, and big boned. I had been told Maurice's long legs were like our father's. I noticed, with interest, that she did not have long legs – just like Charles and me. She had a friendly and open disposition. She was confident. It was clear she bossed her timid and diminutive husband, Uncle Walter, who was so frail that he dragged his feet along with little steps.

We had a warm encounter, and it felt as if we had known her all our lives, though we only knew each other through her occasional correspondence with our mother when I was growing up in Kumasi. During this period, there was the yearly parcel of biscuits from Switzerland at Christmas from her.

Apart from me, everyone at this gathering spoke German. So, when they talked too long, I would butt in in French, because I could not understand them. During this short visit, she wanted to know how our mother was doing and how our life was in Ghana. I was more interested in finding out more about our father, her brother. Maurice hardly asked any questions. Come night time, we were told before eight p.m. that it was time for bed, and we all had to retire. The couch in the living room was prepared as a bed for my boyfriend and me. Maurice and his Swiss girlfriend were given the guest room. Promptly, early the next morning, we all had to get up when she got up. She was the over mothering aunt who reminded each one of us, in turn, to use the only bathroom in the flat.

I learnt from her that our father loved Africa, and that was why she had allowed his body to be buried in Casablanca, where he died on his way back to Ghana. She also mentioned he had been popular with women. She gave me a painting by our father that showed he was a good artist. This influenced me to pick up oil painting, which I enjoy. For the first time, I knew little things like meals he enjoyed eating. She said our father loved to eat, and that rabbit was a particular favourite, so when he last visited her, she prepared that for him. Interestingly enough, my brothers and I do not like rabbit meat. I was to learn with time, in Switzerland, that it was normal to find and buy rabbit and horse meat at the butchers.

This visit confirmed for me that my father was not just a dream. He had existed and was real to not only me – somewhere in my heart – but was always present with his only sister. Sadly, she died of a heart attack shortly after our meeting. Uncle Walter wrote Maurice to inform him after Tante Alice was buried, so we never had a chance to attend her funeral. In this letter he mentioned he was now living with their only child, Gerard, in the Swiss canton of Wallis. Gerard was divorced and had two children. We never met our cousin and lost touch with Uncle Walter after his wife's death. Needless to say, we were all surprised that Uncle Walter would outlive her. She was strong in body and spirit, and he was frail and was over twenty years older than she. It seemed natural that she would outlive him.

Chapter Five: Germany

Getting Married

My family knew I was afraid of marriage. They were right. I have always believed marriage should never be for society's sake, as something to show off. Neither is marriage a meal ticket. It is an institution that needs continuous work. I believe marriage is serious and one of the biggest challenges in life. It is about choosing a partner for life! But what in life is predictable? Matrimony is a gamble. Is the person as whole and balanced as they appear? The most charming person may turn out to be a nightmare to live with. Each person develops individually during the course of their life. Is the development going to bring about changes that are better and not for the worst? What did marriage have in store for me? Was I making the right choice? Was my choice going to last? Was my "Mr Charming" as good as he appeared to be? Was he going to change with time? How many surprises did a life with him have in store for me? Was he going to be there for me when I become weak and old? How was he going to treat me in the long run?

To everyone's surprise, I finally made my decision to marry, at the age of twenty four, only five months after I had met my thirty-one–year-old German boyfriend. He wooed me like no other man before him. He made me feel loved. I felt he sincerely cared a lot for me. He was very focused on me. He travelled from Germany to visit me in Geneva each weekend. We had fun times dining and wining and spent a lot of time just talking. It seemed all we needed was each other. In spite of my plans to go back to Ghana forever, I accepted his proposal.

I was very much aware that this decision meant I would have to spend the rest of my life in Europe. It was for me a big decision. Seven months after being introduced in Zurich by a Ghanaian married to a Swiss, we were married in Ghana. I was the oldest daughter and the first child to marry, so my parents wanted me to marry there. We had a civil marriage in Accra, on 24 December 1976. Our wish for a small wedding was fulfilled, and about thirty people (small by Ghanaian standards) were invited for the reception that took place at my parent's home. For dinner, only very close family members – about six elders of my extended family – joined us at a local restaurant. Uncle Boateng could not help commenting to the waiter, "Don't you people have a kitchen?" upon seeing how his steak was being prepared at the table – flames and all!

The next day, the traditional Ashanti marriage, was less spectacular. There were just family heads, my parents, and a couple of cousins that met at uncle Boateng's house in Accra. Uncle Boateng was then the head of the extended family.

We all sat down and the usual, pretty, simple ceremony was performed. My husband was welcomed into the family. The meaning of marriage was mentioned, and finally, the spirits of our Ashanti ancestors were invoked. Throughout the ages, many people, in all cultures, have believed that the spirit lives on after death. The Ashantis also have this belief. The memory of the ancestors is, therefore, kept alive by mentioning them in all the daily activities, especially during feasts and ceremonies. And so, with the mention of each name, libation was poured. Libation being the slow pouring of schnapps on the ground each time the name of an ancestor or god was mentioned, thanking them for looking after us and asking them to further continue with their good works. Libation was poured to the Almighty God; to the names of the various gods of the Ashanti clan; to the gods of the Ashanti Royal Family; to the names of our dead Ashanti relatives – going as far back as they could remember.

This traditional ceremony was over in an hour. The groom had to pay a small fee – fifty Ghana Cedis – just enough to cover the cost of the schnapps. Normally, the cost of the traditional marriage would have been higher, but the family considered that the groom had borne the cost of the trip to Ghana and the wedding costs of the previous day.

Coping in Germany

A couple of months after the marriage, I left Geneva – with a heavy heart – to join my husband in Germany. He lived and worked in Frankfurt-am-Main. At the beginning, I felt very isolated in this country. For the first time ever, my life was among Europeans only. Gone was the multicultural life I had so enjoyed in Geneva. My first impression of the German language was that I could never speak it. No, I could never pronounce the words, never mind speak the language fluently. I felt at times as if I had been thrown onto another planet. I felt very foreign. I missed the English language so much. Whenever I heard it being spoken, I instinctively moved towards the people. This language gave me a sense of familiarity I was missing badly. My only contact was my husband. He was the only one I knew and could communicate with. He spoke English so it was our language at home.

Going shopping was a challenging task. Counting from one to ten was OK – like in English – but after that, they seemed to count backwards. For example, instead of twenty one, they would say, *Einundzwanzig* (one and twenty); instead of one hundred and ninety nine, they would say, *Hundertneunundneunzig* (hundred, nine and ninety), and so on. This was so confusing to me.

As a result, I could never understand the cashiers at the shops and always checked the screens to find the amount of my bill. This took time and patience. Precisely what the cashiers did not have. Lord help you if you had neglected to weigh an item before bringing it up to the cashier to ring! Laboriously, she would get up from her seat, amble to the produce section, weigh the item, apply the sticker and return and continue her cashier duties. It was best to keep looking forward. That way, you avoided the impatient faces of people lining up behind you at the only open register.

I am happy to say, the customer-business relationship has come a long way since in Germany. I used to be confused as to which came first, the business or the customer? The attitude in business has changed so that businesses actively seek the customers for their business. Catch words like "customer satisfaction" and "service" are common today. Now, a customer is likely to be greeted with eye contact and a smile while receiving service at many businesses like grocery stores.

My husband and I decided to wait four years before starting a family. I decided to use this time to work to integrate in the society. I looked for a job. My choices were very limited because I could not speak the language. I had a Ghanaian passport and needed the appropriate papers to work in this country. The days of getting a German passport automatically after marriage were over. One now had to have been married for five years to be able to apply for a passport. I was only two months in Germany and wanted to work badly. I was bored and lonely. My social life was very limited, and keeping a small flat clean was not enough to keep me busy. With my independent spirit, I wanted to work and earn my own money.

I recall going for my work permit. I waited all morning in apprehension in the corridor full of foreigners. It was finally my turn, and I was called by a female government clerk. She must have gotten up from the wrong side of the bed that day, for she was as mean as a snake and most unfriendly. She was curt and snappy and rattled on in German as fast as she could, talking down to me. It was evident I could not follow her, but she did not care. I was humiliated and felt I must have shrunk a few feet or more. I got the work permit. It was my marital right to get working papers, so she was doing me no favour. I set off for home. My husband wanted me to call him at his office and let him know of the outcome. There were no mobile phones then, so I went into a nearby telephone booth and called him.

His first question was, "How was it?"

I just burst into tears and wept bitterly. I could not get a word out. In no time, there was banging on the door of the telephone booth demanding I get out. Someone else wanted to make a call. Well, I left the booth immediately and continued on my way home, thinking about my encounter and my future in this land.

Not being able to speak German, I went to the employment office of the United States Army in Frankfurt and got a job as a secretary. I immediately enrolled myself in the Inlingua School of Languages and had German twice a week, in the evenings, after work. I read everything I could get my hands on in German and watched German TV to help me master the language. The salary at the US Army was low and the chances for a non-American to advance in the system were nonexistent. I got frustrated. After seven months and with basic German knowledge, I left and started working for the Barclays Bank in Frankfurt.

Prior to this, my husband and I had started a business in which we were doing bazaars at the various US Army bases in the country. This was the beginning of our business career. During the week, we had our jobs and weekends were bazaar days. We sold German gift items like pewter, crystal ware, porcelain products, stuffed animals, and nutcrackers. We imported gift items like the David Winter miniature cottages from England. We also sold imported gift items from Taiwan. We sold products for every pocket!

I was the only black person working at Barclays Bank. The job was very demanding, but the pay was good. The atmosphere was not that great. British manager-trainees commented on how snappy and rude some German colleagues were. They rarely allowed one to explain oneself if there was a misunderstanding. They seemed to enjoy riding roughshod over others. My Ghanaian and British upbringing made me more polite and appear hesitant to them. I never could blow my own horn, and tending not to complain, I ended up getting more and more work. On the other hand, if my colleagues got more work, they would fuss and complain and thus be relieved of the extra work. This all came to a head one day when I decided I had finally had enough. Hiding in the toilet and sobbing was going to get me nowhere.

I noticed my German boss treated my German colleagues with respect and deference. He did not treat me in the same manner but chose, at times, to shout at me. One day, I responded in kind and told him in a loud voice that there were no dogs around and he was to talk to me as a human being with respect, otherwise I was prepared to leave. He was speechless. After this he was very careful towards me, and when I finally left the bank, after the birth of my child, he came to visit me with flowers, asking me to come back. I could not accept his offer because my husband and I had decided I would stay home after the birth of our son. My husband had been working for an English machine company. Unfortunately, it went out of business shortly after our son's arrival. He started working full time in the small family business from home and wanted me to work with him because we could not afford to pay for the extra help.

Our son, Edgar, was born in July 1981. He was my pride and joy, my sunshine, my happiness. He was my life. He was such a happy and contented child. His laughter made me forget the world around me. I believe becoming a mother was the greatest joy I have ever experienced. When he arrived, I instantly knew the unconditional love of a mother for a child. He brought a new dimension and richness to my life. It was wonderful to watch him grow, and time seemed to fly by so fast.

In 1983, we moved from our rented home in Frankfurt to our own house, in the small village of Spiesheim in the state of Rheinland-Pfalz. This meant going from a big city to a village with a population of six-hundred inhabitants. The dusty road in front of our house was not tarred for years, and our son being an outdoor person, came home each evening extremely tired, covered in dust, and wanting to go to bed immediately – without a bath. I would march him to the bathroom, and his pleas to have the bath postponed to another day, met with deaf ears. For Akosua Kyem's granddaughter bathing daily was a must and cleanliness an obsession. He could not escape a daily bath!

I was the only black person in this village and a novelty. All eyes were watching us. These country people were very curious about how I lived my life. I was always bombarded with questions, and yet, I noticed that whenever I asked them the same questions, they did not want to answer. It was clear they wanted to protect their space and privacy. I was in the minority and I had to integrate to survive, so I made no waves and just managed my life. Whenever I walked through the village with my toddler son, I was aware of eyes watching me through curtains from the homes around.

Now that I was working at home, I really missed the company of adults in a big firm. My life was now being there for my child, running the house, and working in our small family business. My isolation made me work even harder for I needed to keep my sanity and stay above things.

Our family business was taking off as we tirelessly worked shoulder to shoulder. Initially, the gift line was our main business. We rented a shop in Mannheim. The only staff we could afford were the sales girls. We sold directly through this gift shop at Mannheim and also through wholesaling to other German shops that were near US military bases, in Kaiserslautern, Rhein-Main, Ramstein, and others. We also took care of the management, purchases, bookkeeping, storage, deliveries, and advertisements. I unpacked all deliveries of gift items we had ordered and neatly put them on shelves to make it easier for me to pack them again when orders arrived from our customers. Yes, we had sales girls who ran our shop, but I had to sort out what they needed and deliver them.

I recall one winter day delivering gift items to our customer, *The House of Clocks*, in Kaiserslautern. On my way back home, I got caught in a heavy snow storm. I had never driven in snow or ice before. In no time at all, the sign posts were covered in snow and it quickly turned dark. I lost my orientation. I drove on and on, at a low speed of 20 km per hour. Traffic on the autobahn was heavy because this was the time that most working people drove home in the evenings. Impatient and over confident drivers trying to overtake the slow moving heavy traffic went off the roads. After what seemed like an eternity, I finally saw a petrol station and pulled in there to ask for directions. There were no navigation systems in cars then. I was told I had missed my exit and had to find my way back. Well, how I made it back home was a miracle to me. But a journey of one hour had taken me at least six hours to complete in this snow storm. My car was intact but packed in about twenty centimetres of snow. I was not hurt and had a lesson on driving in snow and ice. But the next day's news revealed I had been very lucky because the conditions had caused many accidents and deaths. The total damage ran into millions of Deutsche marks, the currency then in use in Germany.

We had also started selling precision steel, but the going was tough. It was initially a side line that took many years to really take off. I helped sort out the steel on the shelves and sent out packages through the post office to the customers. I also prepared the invoices.

We could not afford to employ any house help either, so I worked around the clock.

My day usually started at four a.m. with just a cup of tea for breakfast. Starting early enabled me to work in the office in peace before other chores and demands engulfed me. There were no computers then, so I typed our invoices to our customers – some as many as ten pages and more. I then cross-checked them. Then, I used the adding machine to total the amounts. I cross-checked the amounts from the paper print-outs of the adding machine. I also dealt with our banks and paid all business and private bills. I checked all incoming invoices to make sure we had received all that was billed. I dealt with customer complaints and demands.

Later in the morning, after ten a.m., my son would wake up, and he would need my care and attention. In the course of the day, he wanted me to play with him, and I did. We went bicycle riding, played football, tennis, hide-and-seek, and games. We visited the playground daily. We went swimming. He could interrupt me at any time to read to him, just to talk, or just to sit on my lap in the office and draw. My son accompanied me everywhere because I had no help at home. In addition to these activities, I, of course, attended to our business. My husband was often on business trips purchasing new gift items, visiting our steel suppliers, or calling on our various customers. I was, therefore, often alone, managing our business, child, home, and garden. I ended Edgar's day through bedtime stories and a recount of how he had spent his day. Bedtime meant story telling – seven days a week – fabricated by me or read in English and German. My acting days at St Louis Secondary School came to good use here. I acted and dramatized my stories. Living in Germany, I knew he would end up speaking the language like a native, but I also wanted him to be able to speak English. So, bedtime was also time for learning English, in a playful way, so it would be fun with lots of laughter. Today, I communicate with my son in both English and German.

I would then leave his room for my office to complete the day's work till midnight. I went to bed only to wake up again at four a.m. I was therefore working seven days a week. Life was just work, work, without much fun or break.

In raising my child, I learned a lot about some German people and their ways. I was able to be involved in his world through the playground, sports, and school. I often overheard German mothers encourage the *ego* in their child, underlining the ego and selfish streak in a person. There was a constant comment to the child, "You have to put your foot down or it is your fault if you are at the losing end". To me, the seed of their pushiness and at times their seemingly cold nature is sown at this early stage. I never heard a parent say to their child, "Put yourself in the other's shoes".

We lived right next to the playground. Being very friendly, lively, and generous, Edgar made friends easily. He often supplied other children at the playground with biscuits and drinks. His explanation to me was, "Mama, they are hungry". Our home was, therefore, always full of visiting children.

Not all neighbours in our village had the same sense of openness or fair play. One time I observed – at the playground – a six-year-old girl continuously hitting my three-year-old son with her mother standing by and doing nothing to stop it. This mother studiously turned away! I rushed up to them and told the little girl in front of her mother that if she repeated what she did I would hit her in turn so she would get to know how that felt. The mother turned beet red. She and her family never spoke to me again. My son was never hit again. After this incident, it was rumoured in our village that I was a very protective parent and would take no nonsense where my child was concerned. That reputation was all right with me.

Ever involved in my son's upbringing, I recall being chosen to represent the mothers in the kindergarten. I was the first foreigner ever chosen and the only parent to be chosen for a second year. I seemed to have earned the confidence of the teachers, and they would open up to me about their trials and problems. At one point, the seemingly tough head teacher wept in my arms in her office.

The staff encouraged mothers to spend a morning with their children in kindergarten from time to time. So, I would, sometimes, spend a morning with my son in kindergarten. At least half the children in his class joined my group. Each child wanted to sit next to me. I truly enjoyed these times and moments, seeing the world through the eyes of the children. I loved their innocence.

Edgar was a very active and sportive child. He enjoyed football, tennis, swimming, and athletics. He belonged to many sports clubs in the neighbouring small towns. These clubs were up to the parent to choose. I was his driver seven days a week because there was no public transportation. At sport competitions some parents could not help displaying their ambitions for their children. A football (soccer) match between four year olds – who did not quite understand the rules of the game – was for me comical to watch. For many parents, however, it was serious business!

I remember watching one tennis match in which Edgar's opponent was the team trainer's son. The match was important because it was to determine their ranking in the team. Edgar was about eight years old. I took my place at the farthest bench and calmly sat down to enjoy the match. Suddenly, I witnessed something extraordinary. It had no place in fair play and no place in sports. Edgar was winning, so the trainer started shouting words of support and encouragement to his son. The next thing I knew, the whole crowd was behind them. Edgar, who was winning, was rattled and started to make mistakes and began losing. Tears were welling up in his eyes. I could not believe the scene. With a determined gait, I made my way closer to the court, my arms raised with balled fists pumping the air and yelling loud enough so Edgar could hear me above the crowd, "Edgar, show them! You can do it!

You can beat him! You can win! You're the best"! He heard me and he won that match and many more.

Edgar was adventurous and independent. He was impulsive and did not always come straight home after school. He would choose, at times, to stop at some schoolmate's home to play. I often combed through the village, looking for him. I now understood how my grandmother had felt.

My son was also known for his good appetite. The only difference between him and Auntie Sophia was that he was fussy. His chubby baby feet reminded me of Auntie Sophia's. Today, as an adult, he is still very sportive and determined. His good sense of humour and hearty laughter has remained. But his appetite is under control.

In the 1980s and 1990s, the German school system discouraged mothers from working away from home. It was important for me to put the family first. I was, I believe, a good wife and an even better mother. The greatest reward for me was my child writing me little notes of, "You're the best mother in the whole wide world", and eventually, as an adult, stating that he had had a wonderful childhood.

Living in a German village in the 1980s and 1990s was not easy for a foreigner. I am happy to say the new generation of my son's friends are more open and worldly. The younger generation is more relaxed and not so critical of people of other races and their different ways of looking at life and doing things. In general, however, I find people are alike once the barriers are broken. Being a dog owner, I did make friends with a German lady – also a dog owner. Our warm, uncomplicated relationship has remained to this day.

I have always been driven by focus. I came from a very easy African life to settle in a more difficult and developed world. I felt vulnerable, but I had to make it. So, I did what I always could do best – I stayed focused. I knew I had to manage and survive here for my child if he had to make it here and call it his home. I, therefore, saw myself as a pioneer, just like the first settlers of America. For me, after the birth of my child, there was no road leading back home to Ghana.

Edgar and his mother

Parenting

Motherhood taught me a lot about life. I believe parenthood is a very individual choice. It is also a personal honour. It is a blessing and a joy, intensified when there is stability in one's emotional and financial state. Parenting means being constantly on the lookout for your child's interest and protection. It is a deep learning phase that no books could ever teach or explain. It is a challenge that forces the acknowledgement that, with regard to raising a child, no one has all the answers. Each child is different.

I also believe the love between a good parent and a child is unique. It is love that cannot be replaced. It forces parents to reach their limits in giving their all. You become vulnerable. You feel your child's pain at a level you have never known pain before. His tears cut through your guts. His laughter is your joy. A child is the only *boss* in the world who does not need to speak to get the parents around him or her to do what he or she wants with the sole purpose of seeing that contented smile. The child's smile is your reward, your happiness.

In 1996, I took my son on a two week visit to Ghana. I wanted him to get to know this part of his heritage. I also wanted him to get to know the beauty of the people. Many endure a lifetime of hardships due to a lack of opportunities. However, among these people, a smile is never far away. They are friendly and welcoming to visitors and strangers.

Ghana was for him, at first, a cultural shock for he had never been to a developing country before. The unpaved roads, shabby homes in the ghettos, poverty, poor sanitation, and litter were something he had not expected. As a preventive measure against burglary, most homes have bars across the windows and behind the doors. This was unlike Germany and led him to comment, "This is like living in prison".

Chapter Six: Tracing my Swiss Roots

Since 2004, I have been living in Switzerland. It had always been my wish to trace my Swiss roots. I now finally managed to take time to trace my father's roots. I wanted to walk on the paths and soil where he had walked as a boy in his home town of Balsthal, Switzerland. So, on one cold foggy day in November 2005, I set off by train and arrived there around eleven thirty a.m.. I had to change trains a couple of times, and the trains initially were very modern, but about an hour before I arrived at Balsthal, the trains I boarded looked older. The stations were old too, and I sensed I was moving towards a more remote region of Switzerland.

Balsthal is in a small valley in Canton (State) Solothurn. It is very quiet and hidden – the last stop for the trains. The train station at Balsthal was old. Arriving here on a public holiday gave me the impression that it was a ghost town, not unlike the American western movie, *Once Upon a Time in the West*. The town of more than five-thousand inhabitants is, however, not that small by Swiss standards. It is self-sufficient with all the necessary shops, schools, kindergarten, council, mayor, fire brigade, and so on.

Balsthal is one of the oldest towns in Switzerland. Its history goes back over 4,000 years. The first inhabitants were Celts. The people of Balsthal are said to be sportive and culturally oriented. Like most of Switzerland, it has many walking paths. Before leaving for Balsthal, I checked it out on the Internet. I noticed there is a mountain here known as Mount Brunner. My heart skipped a beat. Was it named after an illustrious ancestor? I never found out.

I strolled through the streets in the town doing sightseeing. I then went back to the train station to catch my train. I had an hour and a half to kill, so I decided to go for lunch in a restaurant near the station. I walked in. It was old but clean and almost empty. The owner and his wife looked at me with an expression that said, "Where did she come from?"

I asked myself, *Are we back in old Apartheid South Africa, or are we in Ku Klux Klan country?*

They were obviously not used to people from other cultures, never mind people from outside Europe! I took a seat by the window facing the train station and asked for the menu. I felt her discomfort. I tried to break the ice by engaging her in conversation, in German, explaining that I had wanted to visit the town and council halls – as my father was from Balsthal. I noticed her warming up, and for the first time she smiled at me and was friendly. Later, I caught her discretely explaining to her husband who I was. Like a typical Swiss, she asked me no questions and gave me no information but just said to come again the next day when the town and council halls would be open.

I left Balsthal happy to have made this journey and planning to return at a more opportune time. It was for me a happy and interesting day with a mixture of feelings about my heritage.

It had taken me over fifty years to get to know the other part of this heritage, a yearning I always had, even as a little girl. I was finally living the unspoken dreams and wishes of a lifetime. After this visit, I got in touch with the authorities in Balsthal and got a print-out of my family tree, which went as far back as 1845. I could even have gone farther back. My father's father, Albert, was from Balsthal, and his mother, Julie Louise, was from Chiesaz in the Canton of Jura, which is French speaking.

My father is said to have spent his formative years in Bienne, Canton Bern, before going to Ghana. Naturally, in my quest to retrace his footsteps, I decided to check it out. I spent a night there as part of a two-day tour of this region. I found it an ordinary industrial Swiss town. It left no impression on me. For some strange reason, I did not feel his presence here.

Today, I have closed this chapter of my life. This is an interesting and historical part for me. Carl Albert Brunner, my father, had had a short life. I thank him for giving me my life – his genes. I can now peacefully live the rest of my life knowing who I really am. I feel fulfilled.

I have also taken advantage of my presence here to get to know my father's homeland. Having eaten chocolates from many parts of the world, I can safely say that the Swiss make the best chocolates. I find the Swiss also bake the best bread and make the finest cheeses in Europe. I have eaten the famous Swiss cheese dishes like fondue and raclette. Fondue is melted cheese eaten from a common bowl into which bread is dipped. Raclette is cheese melted at table and eaten with potatoes. These cheese meals are usually accompanied with white wine and finished off with schnapps. Rösti – fried, grated potatoes, at times with cheese added – is eaten as a side dish. I find these meals nice but rather heavy. Today, I wear a Swiss watch, and it is one of my prized possessions. It has never broken down.

Driving through Switzerland by car, bus, or train, I could not help noticing the picturesque beauty of this mountainous country. The towering magnificent Alps are beautiful to behold, but make you feel insignificant in the greater scheme of things. The mountains dwarf the villages in the valleys. Personally, I found it threatening. I felt hemmed in and claustrophobic, standing in one of the villages. I admired the villagers for not sharing my discomfort.

Compared to other countries, like Germany, towns are relatively small. Towns are usually only a couple of thousand people, and yet each town has its own mayor and council. Skiing being a normal sport, there are ski slopes to be found in many smaller and remote areas. The good, but relatively narrow, roads and accessibility public transportation, like the bus and train systems, reach every corner of this small rocky country.

The Swiss are often criticized by foreigners as being unfriendly in Switzerland. I find the Swiss are down to earth. They tend to be very practical. They are usually very conservative and do not embrace change gladly. They are reserved. The Swiss often wait for the outsider to reach out first to them, and to prove first that they can be trusted. They are usually open, when you make the first move and will encourage you to join them in their activities, but visiting privately is usually not desired. Generally, they seem paranoid about inviting people to their homes. Should you, the stranger, make the first move, they come up with all sorts of excuses to avoid visiting homes. On the other hand, should they make the first move to invite you, there is a shyness and humbleness about their approach. It does not appear to come easily. It seems they fear rejection. This is because they have been raised to be cautious and wait till it is safe to open up. Generally, they appear distant, but when you get to know them, they open up more than a German would.

I remember going on a bus trip from Switzerland to Tuscany, Italy. I entered the bus aware I was the only foreigner. I greeted them, and there was silence. No one answered. But, I noticed how the men quickly glanced at their wives. It was obvious they were all unsure. My friendly, casual way was

177

something they were not used to, and so they did not know how to take it. By supper time, the ice was broken, and both men and women were very friendly and helpful throughout the trip.

Chapter Seven: Looking Back

My last visit to Ghana was in May 2008. It was a trip with my friend Beatrice Aboley-Friebe and her daughter, my godchild, Ilvy Friebe. Beatrice had never visited Ghana since she left after high school for the United States. I knew she wanted and needed to go back to her roots. And yet, in our conversations she seemed to put things off. She seemed to be afraid. Time had made her very foreign to her heritage. She felt no ties to go back to after losing her parents at a very tender age. She remembered her people – vaguely – but they were strangers to her. Some were unknown to her. Besides, she did not speak their language well. She barely understands it. Fact is, being able to speak a language helps connect better. It makes one less foreign.

Beatrice married a German and their only child, Ilvy was raised in Germany. Ilvy was now twenty seven and was curious about her black heritage. To cut a story short, between Ilvy and me, this "trip of a lifetime", as she puts it, was possible.

My own knowledge of Ghana, before this trip, was of only

parts of the coastal area and parts of the Ashanti region. Other parts of Ghana had never really interested me. They seemed so far away. They seemed so foreign. Beatrice said she would only go if I accompanied them. I promised her I would do so on Ilvy's first trip to Ghana. I felt responsible to help them. Besides, it was a chance for me to get to know more about Ghana. My previous visits to Ghana had given me a certain sureness of how to handle my life there. I have always kept contact with some of my relatives and some of my friends, especially Beatrice Appiah-Kusi, who was now working at the Ministry of Tourism.

The African continent is beautiful, interesting, and fascinating. It seems innocent and raw in many ways. Africa has been described, in the past, as "the sleeping continent". It is far from sleeping today. It is hungry and developing. It can also be dangerous in many ways. It can be unsafe at times for foreigners and people, like us, who had become, somewhat, foreign to this land. Besides, we were three women who looked foreign to its people. We were foreign to them in appearance, body language, and speech. There are many languages in Ghana. But I only speak Twi. To people here, it sounded like I was speaking English, I was told. I seemed to have lost the authentic accent after years of not using it often. Besides, my vocabulary had become limited for sheer lack of practice.

I set out an itinerary for this trip, and Beatrice Appiah-Kusi helped us by booking us into relatively good hotels in the various regions as we made our way from Accra in the south to Bolgatanga in the north. Arrangements were also made for us to have a good, rented, four-wheel drive car (because of the bad roads), with air conditioning and the company's own experienced driver. Dealing with a good rental company is very important if you want to ride in a safe car and arrive on schedule, seeing that this trip was for only eight days.

Luckily, Beatrice Appiah-Kusi was at the Kotoka International Airport in Accra to meet us in her old, reliable, two-door, red car, with no air conditioning! The humidity hit us. It was like being in a sauna. We checked into our hotel and ordered cold drinks. It felt sticky from the humidity, and I decided to have a shower. The tap dripped pitifully throughout my showering. It dawned on me this was how it usually was in Ghana – water shortages!

The next day, we toured Accra in Beatrice Appiah-Kusi's good, old, red car. Later, we had a reunion – at our hotel – with some of our old schoolmates that Beatrice could drum up together. It was a warm experience. We recalled past experiences at St Louis and laughed heartily. We also brought one another up to date about our lives. Important in Ghana, we found out that we are all mothers today, and it was interesting to note that unlike our parents, our generation had had fewer children. Most of us had one or two children.

Then we left for Kumasi, the next morning. It was as usual, a bright sunny day. The road to Kumasi was partly tarred and partly not. The latter was still under construction and was a gravelled red path with lots and lots of pot holes.

We passed by many very poor villages with mud houses roofed with straw or tin sheets. There were also roadside stands with people, mainly women, trying to sell produce from their farms. Some walked barefoot and some had on flip-flops, as in the past. We stopped by one of these stands and purchased some plantain and two gallons of palm oil (red oil won from the red seeds of palm trees) to be given as presents. This is a practice I recalled my mother doing, and I felt it appropriate to do so.

Approaching Kumasi, we noticed how many buildings had cropped up in the neighbouring villages close to St Louis Secondary School. Many of these buildings were unfinished constructions. This is because people here tend to build bigger buildings than they can afford. Over calculating one's financial state is often a problem. The result is people can't live in them, if there is no roofing. Without roofing, they are often abandoned.

At last, we reached our old school – St Louis Secondary School. We drove slowly through the compounds, recollecting old memories. I recalled my days as dormitory prefect and the president of the Debating Society. We were pleasantly surprised. The school was not run-down. There were a couple of new buildings, and the compounds were properly fenced in with concrete cement walls, unlike the wired fences of our time. The old trees on the compounds were flowering and looked majestic and beautiful.

We slowly drove out of St Louis and visited our old school matron in Kentenkrono, a village nearby and closer to Kumasi. Matron had aged. She now lived a lonely life with her three dogs that did not look too healthy. She talked of the past and her present life. Tears were shed. Before leaving we gave her a bundle of plantain (cooking bananas) and some money.

We finally checked into our hotel. Ilvy was suffering from stomach cramps, so I advised Beatrice to stay with her daughter at the hotel while I went with our driver, Patrick, to visit those relatives of mine in Ashanti New Town and those living in my mother's former house in Krofofrom. Maurice now owns this house. It was bought by him from his siblings after our mother's death. He generously lets these relatives and their children stay there free of charge while he picks up the bills.

Patrick and I headed for Krofofrom. Our vehicle moved slowly through the overcrowded streets. The place was packed with people and various vehicles all bullying their way through this congestion. People were dressed colourfully. Women had artistically braided hairdos. Many wore wigs in this heat! Some had on head kerchiefs or headgear. It was extremely noisy. People, both men and women, were shouting and dancing in the streets. I asked Patrick what was going on and he told me the popular football club of the Ashantis, Asante Kotoko, had just won the match against a Nigerian team. Yes, I thought to myself, Ghanaians are still football crazy!

We finally reached the road in front of our childhood home. I panicked. Patrick patiently drove up and down this road many times. So much had changed since I left. Many buildings had since sprung up, choking each other for space. The forest reserve is long gone, I found out. It is now replaced by a large and busy crossroad. The area is now very loud and busy as compared to the days of our childhood, when our home was surrounded by empty bushy plots and snakes and lizards were our neighbours.

At long last, I recognised our childhood home now roofed and hidden between so many buildings around. We drove through the gates and Patrick waited for me. Akua Nimah, our old beloved nanny and relative, rushed to meet and hug me. She and the others were surprised at my visit but happy to see me. We talked some. Like always, I gave them money, as is the tradition. I also gave them a gallon of palm oil and a bunch of plantain. I noticed they have now turned the old big garden and garage into a kindergarten. I spent a short time with these kids and offered them sweets from Germany, which they preciously held in their tiny palms before eating them. They stared at me with their big black eyes and curled up eye lashes. The young male teacher also eagerly took some of the sweets. I wished I had had more to offer, but the European airlines' twenty kilogram luggage limit to Ghana made it impossible for me to do so. I was going to spend three weeks in Ghana.

Sadly, I learned from my relatives, that my cousin, Osei Yaw was dying and had been admitted to the Central Hospital in Kumasi, known locally as Gee. Having left Ghana so, so long ago, I had forgotten my way about. A relative was only too glad to jump into my luxury car and have the pleasure of surprising more relatives visiting Osei Yaw.

As we drove to Gee hospital, I observed the surroundings. Things had surely changed. The area seemed very crowded. More houses had sprung up. They seemed chaotically placed, and I guessed they had been allowed to build without much regulation or planning.

The roads to Gee hospital were also very congested. There were many vehicles. Many were too old, polluting the air. There was the usual honking of horns. There were too many people, all bullying their way through the heavy traffic. It was noisy. I noticed our beloved zoo was gone. I asked what happened and I was told, "No money". I recalled how we had frequented this zoo as kids. Animals fascinated us, and we loved and enjoyed watching and observing their moves. The monkeys were our favourite. What a pity, I thought.

I was saddened at the poverty once more. Gee hospital, had surely had some additions, but it was obvious, that they needed more buildings, staff, medication, and much more. Many sick people lay or sat in queues from the parking lot to the wards.

I asked my relative what was going on, and she explained they were waiting to be called in but that there were so many of them that it was impossible for the doctors to see them all that day. Most of these weakened people waited all day long in the blazing sun, knowing that they stood no chance of seeing the doctor that day. Their only hope was that they would be given numbers, on some piece of paper, at the end of the day, that gave them hope of a chance to get closer to the wards the next day and hence a chance to get closer to help they needed badly.

While Patrick waited by our car at the parking lot, my relative led me inside a hospital building. Finally, in one of the corridors we found my surprised cousins (siblings of Osei Yaw) who were waiting to be allowed to visit him. The place was overcrowded. All eyes were watching me. I seemed to be the centre of attention. I tried to conform. I waited with my relatives. It was getting late. Eventually, I got impatient because I also needed to get back to the hotel to see how Beatrice and Ilvy were doing. Besides, our very polite and patient driver also needed some rest. I told my cousins we should just walk in to see Osei Yaw, because I was sure the busy staff had overlooked the fact that they were waiting to go in. Sure enough, we could go in.

Inside this ward, the poverty hit me once more. These very sick people lay in their metal beds in an overcrowded, dormitory-like room. Everything looked so old and run-down. Osei Yaw was just skin and bones. His feet were swollen, and he was very weak. He managed to smile weakly at me, and I held his bony hand for the whole twenty minutes visit until we were told to leave.

Sadly, Osei Yaw died a few days before I left for Europe. Unfortunately, I could not attend his funeral. Finding myself in Accra then and running out of time and money, I figured giving his brother, Akwasi Poku – who lives in Accra – some money to help with the funeral costs was better than my presence without financial help.

The Ashantis regard death as a sad loss. But they believe that the dead person is joining the ancestors. Ashanti funerals are usually big social events – a time to show off, especially if the dead person was rich or influential. Tears are shed, and great emotions are displayed. Funerals take weeks and at times even months to organize. The rituals also take at least forty days to complete. As a result, these celebrations take time and can be very costly. Contributing to funerals is, therefore, normal. It is also expected.

We travelled 2,631 kilometres through Ghana in eight days. In Accra, we visited the Accident Centre of the Korle Bu hospital and witnessed the medical staff struggling to treat patients. Basic things were missing. For Ilvy, who had trained as a doctor in the USA, it was overwhelming seeing "chest tubes" being shared between patients, and nurses caring for patients without gloves. We were all filled with disbelief and sadness at seeing what was being done with so little. We also visited the hospital in Duayaw Nkwanta in the Ashanti region, where Ilvy's maternal grandmother had died. This is where her mother's present life began when the American missionary doctors took her in. We then drove to the northern region. As we entered the savannah belt in the north, we saw many poor little villages, thousands of goats, and many termite hills. We saw lots of poverty. Rather inappropriately, in the sea of poverty, in Tamale, we saw a very modern football stadium that must have cost millions of dollars to build. From Tamale we drove on to Bolgatanga, Bea's ancestral home town. We searched for and found relatives that she had not seen since she was a little girl. Ilvy learned about her black heritage and another culture so very different from that of the European. This trip made Ilvy understand her mother's deepest emotions and fears.

We enjoyed Ghanaian dishes like jollof rice, fufu, and yams. We enjoyed the soups with the stink fish. We enjoyed the

People selling by the roadside

Bolgatanga Market

The Elmina Castle

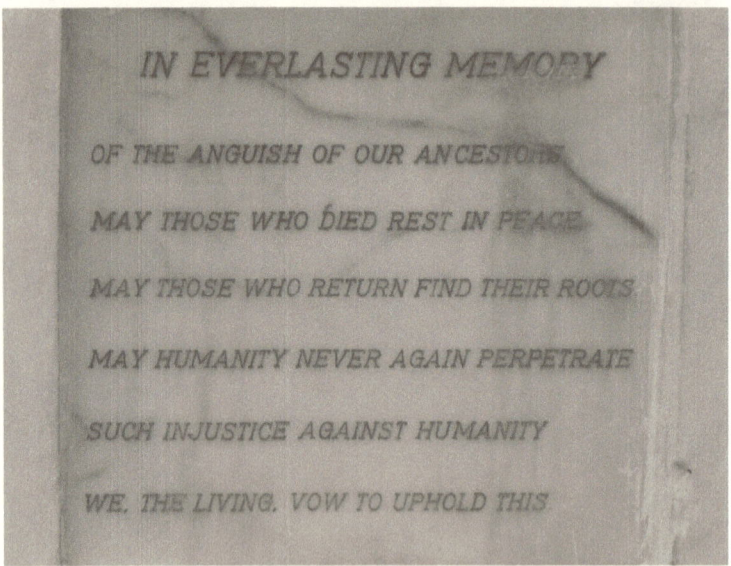

Reference to the Slave Trade, Elmina Castle.

tomato sauces with fried beef or fresh fish. We drank lots of Star beer and shared much laughter and even some tears. And, in the end, we enjoyed some of the many luxuries this country has to offer – a rainforest, beautiful beaches, and most importantly, genuine smiles.

We also visited the infamous slave dungeons of Elmina Castle. Slavery has been among people since time immemorial. There are references to it in the Bible and other ancient documents. Our visit to the Elmina Castle was very emotional. This castle is a former slave hold. It is one of the few remaining today. At this castle there were many hawkers at the entrance exercising that Ghanaian enterprising spirit. You had to run the gauntlet of those traders before you could get into the castle. Once you showed the least bit of curiosity about an item, the rest of the hawkers descended on you to show you that they had the best items for sale!

Inside the castle, people milled about the compounds and residences of the colonial rulers. Our articulate and knowledgeable tour guide informed us there were around fifty such forts at the height of the trade as various European nations fought for dominance of the West African coast.

Once you were taken through the dark, musty, slave-holding dungeons, the mood became sombre. As our eloquent guide spoke, I found myself struggling to control my tears. Some people were openly weeping. It was as if you could feel the suffering that took place here. Our guide said 2 million people passed through these dingy, squalid spaces; half of them perished here because of the unhygienic conditions. They had just enough space to stand in chains in their secretions with one very small hole above them that was their only source of light, and air, while they waited weeks on end to be transported across the seas. To me, the slave trade stands as a testament to human greed and arrogance. Both Europeans and Africans were responsible for and guilty of this wrong.

During this visit, I noticed a lot of changes and improvements in Ghana, but some things have stayed the same with the passing of the years. There were a lot of imported items on the market for those who could afford them. Poverty was still rife. Many people barely managed to eke out a living. There were people with no source of income. Some turned to crime; others depended on the extended family. There is no welfare system as in Europe, but the family helps, sometimes. Nevertheless, people seemed content and were busy with their daily pursuits. I was struck by their zest for life and keen enterprising spirit.

A scene in Cape Coast reminded me of how many Ghanaians were forever trying to hustle or diddle others. We drove by a school. It must have been during their recess for the play ground was full of students. Some were playing football. A kicked ball landed on our road, and the car in front of us drove over it and kept going. The ball burst. I felt sorry for the students. I asked our driver to stop so I could give them money to buy another ball. I knew most balls here were cheap, most likely Asian products. The students must have sensed my intent for they quickly came and surrounded the car. I asked for the price of the ball and, even at that tender age, they were haggling over the price of this ball, from twenty-five to thirty-three Cedis. (The Cedi was then about equivalent to the American dollar.) In the end, I gave them ten Cedis. You never saw a happier bunch of students as they thanked me and skipped back to the playground.

Travelling through Ghana, it was common to see children on the roads smartly dressed in their clean school uniforms walking long distances to and from school, often barefooted. It was also normal to see people walking with loads balanced on their heads – on stretches of empty roads – and no dwellings in sight for miles! Long before we arrived at a town or village, hawkers were lined on both sides of the roads, selling their wares. At junctions, traffic usually was at a crawling pace as we manoeuvred through the congestion of other vehicles, people, and domestic animals. Goats were everywhere. They seemed to know where home was, but during the day, they were freed to feed where they could. As a result, vendors of grain had to be especially watchful.

As compared to the years I lived in Ghana, traffic today is extremely heavy in the centres of towns. Moving vehicles still share country roads and some city streets with domestic animals trying to cross. Hawkers also still dash between lanes, offering their items for sale to passengers in the slowly moving vehicles.

The network of roads, at times good, but often full of pot holes, are used by private cars, taxis, buses, timber lorries (trucks), and trotros. Trotros are the most common form of public transportation in the towns. Virtually all vehicles used to transport passengers are decorated with drawings and religious or wise sayings like: No Jesus, No Toy; Heaven Gate No Bribe; No Hurry in Life; No Food for the Lazy. You also see similar inscriptions on articulated trucks and other big lorries.

Bicycles are rare in the southern part of Ghana. In the northern region, however, bicycles are frequently used and are a hazard to pedestrians and drivers. Most of them have defective brakes or no brakes at all. Beatrice Aboley recalled as a child being knocked down by a bicycle in Bolgatanga. She remembered limping all the way home, crying, with bruises and swollen lips. Suing the rider is still unheard of! They could not pay, anyway.

Driving in Ghana, in general, is a feat. At times, it appears there are no traffic rules. Especially in the big towns, there is often chaos because of the congestion of people and vehicles. During rush hour, some drivers are in such a hurry that they seem to take leave of their senses. So, you often find on a single lane two or three cars trying to move abreast. Oncoming drivers from the opposite direction may also try to force their way through. They also may have two or three cars in one lane, trying to move abreast. This leads to gridlock. Tempers become frayed. There is a lot of shouting and swearing, and occasionally some drivers will actually get out and fight. This, of course, brings the whole traffic to a stand still! Amazingly, by eight p.m., the roads are again clear.

Streets still get very flooded during the rainy seasons because the drainage systems are still not good and are at times nonexistent. And because the roads are badly maintained, vehicles avoiding pot holes often drive on to oncoming traffic.

In this balancing act, passengers are tossed from one side of the vehicle to the other.

Many vehicles would not pass the road tests in Germany or Switzerland. Most car tyres are bald. Many car lights are defective. Some even drive without lights at night.

Street lights are rare. Moving in traffic at night, it was normal to suddenly face an oncoming bicycle with no lights, on your side of the road. To compound matters, the riders did not wear reflective clothing.

Patrick, our driver, told us that when vehicles break down in rural areas, it could take months for the wreckage to be cleared. Neither were neon triangle reflectors used to alert one of the broken-down vehicles because they would be stolen if left overnight. During the day, weeds are pulled out from the sides of the roads and placed on the roads to serve as warning triangles. At night, these organic warning signs are not visible to anyone! This makes it very dangerous at night for all vehicles. Visitors to Ghana are routinely advised not to drive at night. Should they have to, they should go out only in the company of a local, experienced driver.

Street maps are hard to come by. I am told they are often outdated and inaccurate. Ghanaians usually find their way about by using well-known streets and landmarks. Because of the chaotic numbering of houses, the postman normally does not deliver the mail directly to the houses, but does so through post office boxes.

I just love the Ghanaian accent and expressions. I also find it interesting and amusing. Your average Ghanaian speaks a mixture of basic English, pidgin English and English translated directly from the local vernacular. The very well educated speak good English; of course, with a Ghanaian accent.

A simple sentence like, "This woman is pretty too much", just means she is very pretty; "Are you dashing me?"– is it a gift?

In addition, Ghanaians are in the habit of adding vernacular tags to English sentences. For example, "Eh, a man like that dea" really means a "man like that". Foreigners expect the word, "dea" to mean more, but it is a Twi word meaning "that". The additional use of Ghanaian expressions like "Wahu" (meaning, "do you follow me" or "you see") or "ehe, ehe, ehe" (a sign of, "go on") after sentences makes the foreigner and many first-time visitors more confused as they wonder what it all means.

Ghanaians also like using pearls of wisdom from the Bible and literature to advertise or name their businesses. Here are a few examples I noticed when I was there: God Loves You Auto Parts; God may Fitting Shop; The Lord is Victory (for a beauty saloon); Don't Mind Your Wife Chop Bar; Always Always Chop Bar. "Chop bar" is the pidgin English for local restaurant.

Many Ghanaians still view time from a different perspective as compared to the western world. They are not punctual. They refer to their unpunctuality humorously as, "Moving by GMT" (Ghana Man Time). Ghanaians do not mind interruptions in their daily schedules. In the Ghanaian lifestyle, people are welcome to visit without appointments as opposed to the European lifestyle where meetings are scheduled privately and professionally. Ghanaians believe that what is not completed today can be done tomorrow, and if it is not done tomorrow, then there will be other tomorrows. There is an Akan proverb that says, *Onipa be yeebi, wambeye ne nyinaa*. It means mankind did not come to earth to complete all tasks. He or she came to do some of it.

Moving On

Today, I feel my early sense of curiosity and adventure has never left me. It has kept me sprightly and young at heart. I still enjoy people and cultures. I read more than I did in my childhood. Fiction has never interested me. Books on memoirs and autobiographies are my favourites. Books on psychology also interest me. Hey, I told you people interest me. I also read the gossip in the magazines! In general, I still enjoy many sports. After years of wondering what the fun was in going hiking or Nordic walking, I have learned to enjoy them too. My fear of heights has deterred me from enjoying horse riding, rock climbing, or alpine skiing. As a result, I have settled down to cross-country skiing. I am not great at it, for I do not feel comfortable on ice. I learnt swimming late and enjoy it. Snorkelling and diving I avoid, because I cannot keep my head under water. I started golfing late and find it challenging.

I have always believed, holding my head high and keeping my dignity is something no one can take away from me. It has been a life of having goals and being focused and disciplined. There were many happy times in my life. There were also hardships, and there were times when I felt complete despair. I have a strong spirit in me, which tends to make me consider and look at the positive things in life. Despite the difficulties and challenges I encountered, I always persevered and kept hope alive.

Today, I feel comfortable and at home in Europe. I even

enjoy the four seasons. Initially, I only appreciated the spring and summer months. The brightness of the days brought life back. Seemingly dead plants – in the autumn and winter – came back to life and started flowering. People wore brighter colours, and they smiled more.

On the other hand, I dreaded the autumn and winter months. Coming from the tropics, I not only dreaded the cold but feared the darkness and fogginess that prevailed often – gloominess overshadowed everything. To me, there was an air of silent death. I called it Dracula weather. Today, I see it as a cosy time of the year. It is, for me, a time of inner pondering and rumination. I now understand why people here constantly talk about the weather. It is unpredictable. Having experienced winter on the mainland of Europe, I also now understand what people meant by when they referred to Britain as having mild winters. In Britain, I could get by wearing autumn clothes in winter. It hardly snowed, too. On the other hand, in Switzerland and Germany, it is cold and icy, and it snows a lot in winter. I am therefore always bundled up in very thick clothes here.

I have been blessed with a healthy and wonderful child. I lead a good life and encounter many good people. I am fluent in English and German. I am proud to say I can also switch back to the Ashanti language, Twi, as need be, with my Ghanaian relatives and friends.

I never planned to live in Europe for a lifetime and call it my home. Africa was my continent and Ghana my home, my motherland. I love Ghana. But life had other plans for me.

This difficult and at times challenging European continent, I was to learn to love and appreciate.

I feel I am a well balanced person with a realistic outlook on life. I know who I am and do respect and appreciate the differences in others. I can work hard, and I can have fun. I appreciate humour and enjoy laughter. The two cultures – African and European – have been generous to me! In the final analysis of my life, when all is said and done, life has been good to me.

www.ingramcontent.com/pod-product-compliance
Lightning Source LLC
Chambersburg PA
CBHW022247290526
45785CB00015B/386